BODY MIND SPIRIT

Tapping the Healing Power Within You

A 30-DAY PROGRAM

Richard P. Johnson, Ph.D.

Liguori

LIGUORI, MISSOURI

Published by Liguori Publications
Liguori, Missouri
www.liguori.org

ISBN 0-89243-450-3
Library of Congress Catalog Card Number: 92-81358

Copyright © 1992, Richard P. Johnson, Ph.D.
Printed in the United States of America
09 08 07 06 05   10 9 8 7 6

Scripture selections taken from the *New American Bible with Revised New Testament*, copyright © 1986, by the Confraternity of Christian Doctrine, Washington, D.C., are used with permission. All rights reserved.

Excerpts from the English translation of *The Roman Missal,* copyright © 1973, International Committee on English in the Liturgy, Inc. (ICEL), are used with permission. All rights reserved.

Liguori Publications, a nonprofit corporation, is an apostolate of the Redemptorists. To learn more about the Redemptorists, visit *Redemptorists.com.*

Cover design by Pam Hummelsheim

DEDICATION

To my brother Thomas A. Johnson, Jr., M.D. — four and a half years my senior.

His dedication to medicine is eclipsed only by his devotion to the people of God, whom he serves in his ministry of primary healthcare. He is a sterling man, a loyal Christian, a loving father, and a model family physician, who teaches virtuous living and loving service to everyone he touches. I am indebted to his balanced example from the day of my birth.

CONTENTS

PREFACE

Jesus said to the disciples of John the Baptist, "Go and tell John what you have seen and heard: the blind regain their sight, the lame walk, lepers are cleansed, the deaf hear, the dead are raised, the poor have the good news proclaimed to them" (Luke 7:22). Healing was an integral part of the ministry of Jesus, and so it is today. The same power that Jesus used two thousand years ago on this earth remains with us still. This book is about how you can tap into this healing power. No, this book is not about so-called "faith healing," in which reliance is placed upon allegiance to a Higher Power to cure your physical ills. It is, however, about how you can gain in strength and wellness on a spiritual level and allow this newfound energy to become a factor in the overall healing system you have within you.

When I speak of sickness, I mean any form of brokenness that the human condition may encounter. This includes not only all forms of disease and any bodily malfunction but also the maladies of the mind, the hurts of the heart, and the savage attacks on the spirit that this world can inflict. *Brokenness* is the term I use to describe any pain of the body, mind, or spirit that causes impairment of any kind. Each of us suffers from brokenness in one form or another. It is into this personal brokenness that Jesus can enter with the healing power of the Most High. It is up to us to invite Jesus in, and that's what this book will help you do — invite Jesus into your brokenness.

Sickness is a fact of our human existence. As one of the four horsemen of the Apocalypse, sickness has ravished humankind since the beginning of time. Yet, today more than at any previous time in history, our culture has developed a most impressive inventory of means to combat sickness of all kinds and to provide cure where there formerly was none. What we sometimes call the good old days were, in fact, times when we were much more vulnerable to pain, pestilence, and pathogens than we are today. Since 1981, I have been director of Behavior Sciences in the Department of Family Medicine in a one-thousand-plus bed hospital. I have seen people from all walks of life come into the halls of this place seeking healing. The degree to which they find what they desire is not simply a function of the medical expertise they find there but is also influenced by other forces within them and from above. This book explores these other forces and outlines a thirty-day plan for tapping into them.

The medical community is just now beginning to understand the vital connections that exist among the various systems of the mind, the emotions, the spirit, and the body. Systems that were previously thought to operate quite independently are now recognized as moving in a grand synergistic symphony and together form the marvelous healing system that lies within you. These new findings are challenging the very way that we conceive and think about what sickness is and how it operates. I am privileged to stand on the shoulders of the many dedicated medical and psychological researchers and practitioners who have worked before me. Many work on still trying to unlock the secrets of healing. I am indebted to and stand in awe of men and women such as the late Norman Cousins, Gerald Jampolsky, M.D., Bernie Siegel, M.D., Larry Dossey, M.D., Joan Borysenko, Ph.D., Stephen Levine, Dean Ornish, M.D., Deepak Chopra, M.D., Wayne Dyer, Ph.D., and Harold Riker, Ed.D. In addition, I would like to thank the wonderful people at Liguori Publications, especially Audrey Vest, whose ability to grasp my sometimes obscure meaning and shape it into written clarity still amazes me. A more capable and well-read editor I could not find.

Richard P. Johnson, Ph.D.
St. Louis, Missouri
September 1992

Chapter One

SPIRITUAL HEALING: OUR NATURAL INHERITANCE

Humanity cannot create love, nor can the world produce peace. Love and peace are gifts from God, and because we are God's children, they are our natural inheritance.

- The Spiritually Healing Person
- The Healing Virtues
- The Mind/Body Connection
- The Motivational Model

The Spiritually Healing Person

At one time or another, each of us has come in contact with someone who seems to rise above grave, painful, or even terminal illness. Such persons know that they have contracted a disease but seem strangely undeterred by it. Accepting their sickness as a challenge, they respond to it not with anger, disgust, or depression but with a transformed zeal and zest for life. They apparently possess an otherworldly understanding of their malady that sets them apart from those of us who react more "humanly." These people, whom I refer to in this book as *spiritually healing,* seem to be "in tune" with something beyond themselves, some force that transcends this material plane. It's almost as if they have received a gift of invulnerability to the otherwise tragic event we call sickness. What power sets these people apart from the norm? What special quality allows them to respond to the tragedy in their lives with such peace of mind and calmness of action? These are the questions that inspired this book.

In the last few pages of my previous book, *A Christian's Guide to Mental Wellness* (Liguori Publications, 1990), I enumerated twenty-four characteristics of what I called "spiritually awakening persons." As I reviewed these, I realized that many could describe the concept of spiritually healing persons as well. These twenty-four characteristics are "virtue based" in that their root motivation is not of this world but comes from God. They are extensions of the love and peace that come only from God. Humanity cannot create love, nor can the world produce peace. Love and peace are gifts from God, and because we are God's children, they are our natural inheritance. As you read the twenty-four characteristics of spiritually healing persons listed below, remember that they are ideals and that this is not an ideal world. They are goals to strive after, targets to shoot for; they give us guidance for living our lives, knowing full well that we can never fully attain them. Let's look at these twenty-four characteristics of spiritually healing persons.

1. They see the good in all things, including the consequences that can be derived from sickness.
2. They are joyful, knowing that God is ultimately "in control."
3. They recognize that mistakes, losses, and "failures" are important points of learning and are therefore blessed.
4. They focus only on reality; they cannot see illusions or deceit.

5. They trust that all is well, even though they cannot fathom exactly how.
6. They live in the "now" of God's love.
7. They know that they never walk alone; God is always present.
8. They recognize God's work in their lives, including their illness.
9. They are God-reliant; they know that God will guide them through their sickness.
10. They patiently wait for God's leadings through their disease.
11. They transcend criticism, even their own.
12. They rejoice in knowing that all people, including their caregivers, are children of God.
13. They seek to be Christlike in all they do.
14. They find peace in all things, even their illness.
15. They maintain a steadfast determination to seek and follow God's plan, not their own, in the face of all adversity.
16. They allow love to pervade their thinking about all people, things, circumstances, and situations.
17. They are kind, gentle, and loving to their bodies.
18. They accept the frailty of humanity and their ultimate strength in God.
19. They surround themselves with amazement and gratitude for God's creation.
20. They find divine revelation in ever-expanding and personal ways.
21. They maintain an attitude of empathy; they "walk" with others.
22. They transform negative emotion into loving decisions.
23. They speak with authority; they cannot argue.
24. They praise God continuously.

The Healing Virtues

During the course of my work with both inpatients and outpatients at a large medical center in a major metropolitan area, I have personally met spiritually healing persons. I have heard nurses speak with excitement and surprise about these unique and captivating people, who seem to defy the natural laws that govern us all. I have witnessed their depth, their peace, their strength. Most of all, I have felt the inspirational force that seems, paradoxically, to set them apart from the rest of us while at the same time pulling something inside of us toward them. Spiritually healing persons inspire an almost irresistible attraction. There is something mesmerizing, compelling, and utterly peaceful about them that draws like a magnet.

I analyzed the twenty-four virtues that constituted the core of the twenty-four characteristics in light of what I was observing in the spiritually healing persons I was seeing at the hospital. What I found was that, while these twenty-four virtues figured heavily in their behavior, they did not explain all the actions, attitudes, perceptions, and feelings that spiritually healing persons exhibited. After further investigation, I added six more virtues to the list. The resulting thirty virtues explained more thoroughly the behavior exhibited by spiritually healing persons. In this book, I refer to these as "the healing virtues."

Thirty-day Healing Retreat

This book is not intended simply to be read. Rather, it is meant to be used as an activity manual. More accurately, it is put together to create a transforming experience for you. It consists of eight chapters. This first chapter serves as an introduction to the concepts underlying the healing virtues and spiritually healing persons. Each of the middle six chapters (chapters 2-7) define five of the thirty healing virtues. For each of the healing virtues, you will find a secular definition and a spiritual description, together with an explanation of how a real-life spiritually healing person came to use or to learn that virtue as a result of his or her sickness. Each day you awaken to a new virtue, a new way of seeing your brokenness, a new opportunity for healing. Each day for thirty days you encounter Christ's miraculous ways, his healing grace, and the soothing balm of his care. A morning, an afternoon, and an evening meditation is also given for each virtue.

In Chapter Eight, I've described ten techniques to help you use the thirty healing virtues as the basis for your thirty-day, self-paced "Healing Virtues Retreat." You may make this retreat on your own in the privacy of your own solitude with God, you may share the thirty days with a friend, or you may even want to form a "Healing Virtues" support group of persons dealing with illness of any sort. More about this group concept as well as other suggestions for augmenting spiritual healing are discussed in the Appendix.

Who are we meant to be? One of my favorite psychologists, the late Abraham Maslow, left us many valuable insights into human nature. One of his cornerstone tenets stemmed from his questioning of why, if we want to know about human nature and the human condition, we insist on studying people who are ill. This logic led him to study not those who were emotionally or mentally ill but rather those persons who represented the best among us. He set out to discover what motivated those who succeeded at the highest levels of accomplishment rather than those who functioned with some impairment.

Maslow's findings have changed the way we think about ourselves and the possibilities we can aspire to. He developed a concept he called "self-actualization" that refers to becoming all we possibly can be. When we become who we truly are, we are self-actualized.

As Christians, we are certainly called by God to become all we can be and to transform ourselves gradually from what this world says we should be to what we truly are. We are called, then, to become self-actualized in our faith. When we are faced with all manner of human tragedies, including serious illness, our Christian heritage motivates us to act as Christ would have behaved in similar situations. We know we can never attain the spiritual heights that he could even in his human form. Nevertheless, Christ beckons us to develop spiritually and become better as a consequence of these tragedies. Gradually, we are called to regard all our earthly experience as blessed in that we can learn to become closer to him through it.

Spiritually healing persons are growing in just such a direction. Naturally, there are as many degrees of spiritual healing as there are individuals. It's not a question of being or not being a spiritually healing person. Rather, it's a question of the degree to which you are growing closer to God and thereby developing a heightened ability to perceive your illness as a holy part of your earthly journey. Here, indeed, is the challenge of your illness!

Could it be, I asked, that spiritually healing persons actually use their illness to propel their journey toward self-actualization and spiritual awakening? Does their illness provide them with a vehicle that has transported them to ever higher levels of spiritual and emotional maturity? If this is so, how does it happen? By what mechanism could the tragedy of sickness catapult these "victims" beyond the confines of what is considered normal? To what degree were they "spiritually awakening," even before they had experienced the misfortune of illness? Were there themes or commonalities that distinguished these inspirational folks? Did they all arrive at this point of growth and awakening by the same means or processes, or did each develop in ways unique to his or her own self? These and other questions became the core issues of my search to find the secrets of how spiritual healing develops.

The Exceptional Patient Popular author Dr. Bernie Siegel, a surgeon at Yale University, coined the term *exceptional patient* to describe persons whose disease has provided them with an opportunity to begin living as they had not been able to live before. He refers to their illness as a "wake-up call" or a "reset button," because they seem to become more fully alive and more fully human as a result of it. Such patients regard their physical malady not as the "kiss of death" but as an event designed to foster their growth.

Obviously, such a perspective is quite contrary to the ordinary view of illness as an unfortunate encumbrance at best or as the final unfair catastrophe of their lives at worst. Among other things, Dr. Siegel urges patients to participate in their own healing and not to fall passively at the doorstep of the medical community like a lamb that has lost its way home. He asserts that patients must become knowledgeable about their illness and aware of their emotional reactions to it at very deep levels if they want to remain involved in their active healing, whether that healing be physical or otherwise.

In the Introduction to his book *Love, Medicine, and Miracles,* Dr. Siegel describes the characteristics of exceptional patients. All their thoughts and deeds advance their cause of life rather than expressing an unconscious "death wish," as Sigmund Freud taught. Exceptional patients take charge of their lives in ways that foster self-esteem, a genuinely healthy and humble self-love. They work hard to love themselves and dedicate their lives to loving rather than judging. They form deep human relationships with their doctors that energize the therapeutic effects of their treatments. They demand to be treated as an individual, not as a disease. Exceptional patients make full use of the life force within them, thinking, feeling, and choosing to extend love in any way they can. They go about finding healing in its fullest sense, not just curing a disease. "Death is not a failure" for exceptional patients, Dr. Siegel reminds us. "Not choosing to take on the challenge of life is."

Peace of Mind The one characteristic Dr. Siegel mentions but spends little time explaining is the one that is central to our beliefs as Christians. Peace of mind is a central goal for exceptional patients who wish not only to live fully functioning human lives in spite of their illness but desire to push beyond the realm of wellness and enter spiritual awakening. Here is the dividing line between exceptional patients and spiritually healing persons. As Christians, we are called to go beyond what the world can offer — in this case wellness — and aspire to the lofty heights of spiritual awakening. God wants us to know him better and better. We are not to be satisfied with our natural humanness (even though we do cherish it); we stretch beyond it into the realm of the supernatural. Here is our mission.

This book is a journey for you, an invitation to experience your life right now in a different manner. This new way of experiencing includes a transformation of your very self. Christ told us we must lose ourselves in order to gain ourselves.

> "Whoever wishes to come after me must deny himself, take up his cross, and follow me. For whoever wishes to save his life will lose it, but whoever loses his life for my sake and that of the gospel will save it."
>
> Mark 8:34-35

This paradox is the fulcrum upon which swings your ability to see your sickness as having meaning and purpose, to understand the value of what's happening in your life, to appreciate your life for what it is, and to be grateful for the gifts you have been given. In short, you are being called to have peace of mind and all that it entails. Here is our quest!

The Mind/Body Connection

Sickness Since the main focus of this book is healing, we need to discuss the reason healing is necessary — sickness. First, sickness is not preordained or prearranged by any celestial power. While allowing sickness to exist on the material plane we call the earth, God does not choose particular people to be the unfortunate victims of it. Having said this, we are confident in our faith that the Holy Spirit can transform any and all earthly happenings into methods for spiritual enrichment. Our bodies are in this world and of this world; therefore, they are governed by the natural physical laws of the world. Sickness is caused entirely by the work of material forces acting in purely scientific and understandable ways on the physical parts of the body.

We are not made to suffer sickness in atonement for the sins of our forefathers or for any other transgression of ourselves or others. Rather, sickness results solely from physical causes: accidents, a history of lifestyle abuses, invasion of pathogens external to the body, or sheer wearing out of the "bag of bones" we call the body. Our bodies do not have minds of their own; they cannot cause us to become sick. They react to the physical forces acting upon them much the same way as a billiard ball reacts by moving away from the force of another ball striking it. A purely natural and material law is at work here.

You may ask, "Well, don't my emotions and my thoughts play a role in the development of disease? Don't overwork and worrying cause ulcers?" The answer to these questions is "Yes and no." While it is true that overwork and worrying (as well as other stressors) exert tremendous pressures on the body, stressors themselves do not cause the sickness.

Ulcers result from an overabundance of acidic gastric secretions gradually wearing (or burning) a hole (or abrasion) through the mucosa lining of the stomach. The fascinating thing is that thoughts and emotions actually cause chemical changes in the body. Worrying (negative thoughts and emotions) in turn stimulates changes in the chemical combinations in the nervous system, which then stimulate other purely physical and chemical reactions to take place. Eventually, these changes greatly increase the levels of gastric secretions. Finally, hyperacidity in the stomach eats away the lining of the stomach wall creating an ulcer.

Sickness is physically based. Our response to it is the result of our emotionally or spiritually driven choices. We cannot stop the sickness from occurring. However, we do have the power to direct the effects of the sickness onto or away from us. As you will see in the ensuing chapters, my investigation shows clearly that we all have the power to become inspirational, spiritually healing persons.

Illness I wish to make a clear distinction between illness and sickness. *Illness* is defined as an unhealthy condition of the body or the mind. *Sickness* is defined as an unsound condition or a specific disease. In sickness, the body is malfunctioning at some level; there exists a breakdown in the smooth operation of this marvelous mechanism we call the body. Illness is the name given to our emotional reactions to the sickness, including the lifestyle and behavioral responses we make as a direct consequence of the imposition of the sickness on our life.

There is little, if anything, you as an individual can do about sickness. You have a disease; it is present and it is running its course. You can rest, take medications, participate in physical therapy, and so forth, but still the progress of the disease or disorder adheres to the material laws of nature.

On the other hand, you do have great control over your illness. You control how you will respond to your sickness. You can be despondent, demoralized, and dependent and act accordingly. Or you can adopt an emotional response of determination, drive, and detachment from the sickness.

Your sickness just happened, caused by purely physical forces. To believe otherwise gives the body control over the mind. It implies that some magic exists that gives matter creative ability it cannot have. The other possibility would be to assume that God consciously and deliberately decided, for whatever malevolent reason, that you deserve to be sick.

Neither of these two possibilities is real; neither is plausible. The physical plane does not hold sway over the spiritual, nor is God a vengeful God. You do not make your sickness. Your illness, on the other hand, *is* of your own making. You design it and you maintain it. To believe otherwise denies your God-given gift of free will, your ability to act as you see fit on this plane. You choose the *responses* to your sickness.

Jesus used miracles to cure sickness and disease. Those who observed these miraculous cures marveled at his power and were awed by the effects. Most of the spectators focused only on the physical event. Some, however, recognized the miracles as Jesus intended — as signs and symbols of even greater healing of spiritual poverty and moral maladies.

Jesus came to extend his spiritual kingdom on earth, not to start a medical clinic. He was interested in the soul, not the body. Yet Jesus was compassionate. When he cured the man of his blindness with mud made from spittle and asked the man to wash his eyes in the pool of Siloam, Jesus was challenging us to use everything physically possible, from medications to specialized therapies, to cure human disease. Miracles are not the only means of curing sickness. We are to avail ourselves of the discoveries and inventions of the medical community. We are not to remain victims of our own helplessness. Jesus used miracles only as adjuncts to the more important work of spirit-building and healing.

Norman Cousins, editor of the *Saturday Review* for almost thirty years and professor in residence at the UCLA School of Medicine until his death, is famous for his pioneering work in the "mind/body" connection. In his book *Head First: The Biology of Hope,* Cousins had this to say about emotions and illness:

> ...illness, physical or mental, could be the result of many things — not just what went into the human stomach but also what went into the mind; relationships with family, friends, and the outside world; ambitions, hopes, or fears. Medical science might not always be able to conquer or ameliorate all these forces....

Even though Cousins tried to write about the mind/body connection with complete scientific objectivity, he could not do so without involving virtues. In *Head First,* he wrote: "What the experts missed was the way the human mind could override statistical evidence in response to deep determination or the anticipation of a loving experience."

Research in the new field of inquiry called psychoneuroimmunology has found that sickness, illness, and healing are all activated by complex reactions and interrelationships within the body and mind involving the brain, the endocrine system, and the immune system. This research is not only fascinating from a scientific standpoint but reveals for the first time that our growth in virtues — our spiritual development — can have direct application to healthy living. A most fantastic finding!

Healing and Cure Just as we need to distinguish between sickness and illness, we must do the same with healing and cure. Healing comes in infinite variety but only two categories: healing sickness and healing illness. For our purposes, healing as it relates to sickness is best described as "cure," recovery or relief from a disease. To cure is to correct, restore to the original, heal, or permanently alleviate a sickness. Cure refers to the functional "fixing" of something that was formerly broken. Cure applies to the physical, material realm alone.

In this book, we will focus on the second category of healing, healing illness. This type of healing refers to making sound or whole, overcoming an undesirable situation, restoring purity or integrity. In this sense, healing includes your willingness to perceive your illness differently. Illness emerges when you become separate from your true self by believing that your sickness violates your genuine identity. Illness causes you to lose faith and trust in God; it renders you broken from him and leaves you feeling a sense of spiritual alienation. When you find yourself in this state of spiritual separation, that is precisely where you need healing.

Healing is a free gift that God promised would be ours through faith. One aspect of faith is the recognition that sickness will not ultimately bring loss, even though, on the physical plane, loss seems the only result of sickness. Faith allows us the vision to recognize our sickness as an opportunity for eventual gain. Healing is a release from the fear that without a healthy body we are lost and helpless. By bringing peace, healing breaks the anger and rage that swell up in the hearts of our unhealed selves.

This peace is the logical emotional consequence of viewing sickness differently and, therefore, thinking cohesively and comprehensively rather than critically and chaotically. Healing allows us to learn our wholeness and holiness and become blessed as we remember that we are sons and daughters of God. The sense of danger, vulnerability, and defenselessness we feel so acutely when we are ill and separated from God is healed as we replace fear with love in our lives through the holy process of healing.

Healing involves opening our ears to hear the soothing communication of the Holy Spirit, whose message is always wholeness. Healing our illness goes beyond the physical to a higher realm where the will of God resides. This type of healing transcends what our physical self would desire and allows the light of love to enter where the darkness of fear had been. Healing is accomplished when we can no longer see value in physical suffering and instead clearly recognize that peace is an attribute that can only be found within. Inner peace is a sure sign of healing and is our natural state when we relinquish control and give it back to God. This is health.

Healing requires our cooperative consent to the healing power within us. Our tireless internal healer constantly nudges us toward God. We must accept the lead of this careful custodian of our welfare and recognize that it is concerned primarily with our spiritual development and our true prosperity. We must be a willing partner in the journey toward wholeness and light by listening to the divine voice within us. This faint but steady and patient inner teacher can be easily drowned out by the emotional poisons of fear, envy, jealousy, anger, suspicion, and so forth.

Prayer is our primary means of listening. Prayer calms the interference that threatens to distort the message and render us alone and helpless. Prayer has transformed many an irritable patient into a healed model of holiness and inspiration to other sufferers.

The Motivational Model

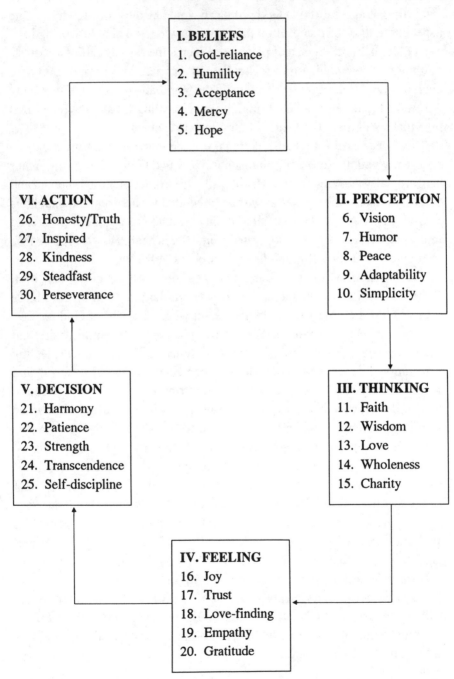

I. BELIEFS
1. God-reliance
2. Humility
3. Acceptance
4. Mercy
5. Hope

VI. ACTION
26. Honesty/Truth
27. Inspired
28. Kindness
29. Steadfast
30. Perseverance

II. PERCEPTION
6. Vision
7. Humor
8. Peace
9. Adaptability
10. Simplicity

V. DECISION
21. Harmony
22. Patience
23. Strength
24. Transcendence
25. Self-discipline

III. THINKING
11. Faith
12. Wisdom
13. Love
14. Wholeness
15. Charity

IV. FEELING
16. Joy
17. Trust
18. Love-finding
19. Empathy
20. Gratitude

The Motivational Model

A **Path to Healing** How can this transformation from human frailty to spiritual vision come about for you? How can you become a spiritually healing person? My goal in this book is not simply to provide a picture of what a spiritually healing person looks like but, perhaps more importantly, to provide a road map to help you get there yourself.

In the first chapter of *A Christian's Guide to Mental Wellness,* I outlined a six-step Motivational Model for growth and development (page 18). It's precisely this model that becomes the vehicle we use in our journey from illness to healing. Let's take a look at each of the six steps. They form the outline of the remainder of this book and are our guide toward transformation. [Editor's note: Readers familiar with Dr. Johnson's *A Christian's Guide to Mental Wellness* will notice that the labels of some of the six steps in the Motivational Model have been changed in the current book. The content of the model, however, remains essentially the same.]

Beliefs The first step in the Motivational Model is *beliefs.* At the very core of our human self, we find a cache of ideas that we hold on to with all our psychological strength. These dearly held ideas are called many names, including beliefs, attitudes, value system, primary assumptions, and expectations. This set of ideas provides us with our central operating instructions for living. We may liken this to the disk operating system used in computers. Even the most sophisticated computer requires such a system to tell it how to run; without this system, the computer would or could do nothing. Beliefs are like operation systems; without them we would simply flounder like a cork in a storm at sea.

Our beliefs tell us what's right and what's wrong; what to value and what not to value; where our priorities are; what's moral, ethical, and righteous and what isn't. Our beliefs provide a sense of relationship with God. Our beliefs are the wellspring, the starting point, for all we think and do. They are what get us up in the morning; they govern interpersonal relationships and tell us whether we're "on" or "off" track.

In Chapter Two, you will see how you can begin to change your beliefs to bring them in line with the healing power of God.

Perception The second step in the model is *perception.* Each of us sees the world in a more or less unique way; no one else sees it exactly the way you do. How we see ourselves, others, relationships, events, and so forth, determines how we will relate to them. How do you see sickness and illness?

We see things at the directives of the beliefs we hold to be true. For example, imagine that you have always lived in a red room and that everything in that room is exactly the same shade of red, even you and your clothes. Imagine that all the food you eat is also the same color; indeed, you have never seen the other colors — no shades or hues, no variation at all. Would you know the other colors? No, you'd have nothing to relate to. You would not believe in the other colors, because they are not part of your belief core. Would you know red? Again, you would not, because you have nothing to compare it to; you would not have developed a sense of color at all.

By the same token, our beliefs about everything in our experience are guided, indeed directed, by our deeply held values and attitudes. When something is presented to us that runs contrary to what we believe, our first reaction may be to deny it because it presents a conflict. We see what we believe.

The apostle Thomas did not want to believe that Christ had come to the other apostles, asserting that he would not believe until he first saw with his own eyes. The idea that a dead man could live again ran so contrary to what Thomas believed that he tried to refute it, insinuating that the others were imagining. Christ's response, "Blessed are those who have not seen yet believe" is the perfect statement of faith in the power of God. It is just such power that lies within us and nudges us to use the healing strength that it offers.

Thinking The third step is *thinking*. After a belief directs us to perceive an event in a particular manner, we are now free to think about what it means to and for us. Our thoughts usually bring us to evaluate the meaning and purpose of this event for us. Our thinking represents how we place this event or relationship into the scheme of our lives as we perceive it.

Although no one can force us to think in a certain way, sometimes we feel trapped into thinking in a particular manner. Persons who follow a certain political, religious, moral, economic, or psychological philosophy are considered as thinking alike. Movements down through the ages have sought to "win" people's minds. The advertising industry is based on influencing our thinking, and it uses every contrivance to do so.

In Chapter Four, we will learn how several spiritually healing persons learned to think about their illness so that they could transcend it.

Feelings The fourth step in the Motivational Model is *feelings*. We are emotive people. We like to feel; indeed, we must feel. When we try to "stuff" our feelings, we are almost guaranteed to suffer some consequence, because feelings eventually will be expressed. If we do not or cannot express them clearly, directly, and healthfully, repressed feelings will find other, not so healthy, ways of finding expression. These negative ways usually make us sick.

Stuffed feelings do not just stay stuffed; they have a tendency to leak. They can leak into our joints, our heart, our lungs, our pancreas, our bowels, and so forth. They can also leak into our emotions in ways that may eventually produce depression, anxiety, or some other affective disorder, such as compulsions, addictions, or phobias. Our feelings about our sickness will determine to what degree we are able to maintain emotional equilibrium throughout its course.

Decisions The fifth step, *decisions,* follows from feelings. Feelings motivate us to consider alternatives. Sooner or later, however, we must choose what we will do. Once we have experienced enough emotion, we eventually decide that something must change, that this pain is unbearable, and we exercise our free will.

As Christians, our job is to align our will with God's will. This is no easy task, for it requires that we listen deeply to that fragment of the Father within us. The first rule for decision-making is to make no decisions alone; always consult God first, asking what Christ would decide in such a situation. Sometimes the answer is surprising, for it moves us to exercise tough love.

Chapter Six invites you to examine the decisions you have made concerning your life right now and to expose them to the clear light of Christ's love. In addition, Chapter Six relates a stirring story of a spiritually healing person who has confronted the alternatives of her present life and has chosen God clearly as her co-director.

Action The God we know as Christians is a God of *action,* the sixth and final step of the model. We are called to do, to operate, to act in this world. We are called to perform God's work here. We are called to become teachers in God's kingdom. With renewed attitudes and beliefs, clarified perception, healthy thinking, examined feelings, and considered choices, our job is now to *do.*

Translating the other five steps in the Motivational Model into a coordinated action that is faithful to God's Word allows us to tap into his healing

Power and to teach only love in our actions. Chapter Seven reveals the love actions of a true spiritually healing person who has absorbed the challenge to act in the face of her own sickness, which at first seemed a contradiction of God's promise of life in abundance to her.

Let's Begin! The six steps of the Motivational Model provide for us the essential framework for our conversion from disgruntled and disillusioned patients whose sickness has made us ill into glorious spiritually healing persons for whom sickness has become a challenge and an opportunity for healing. Our trek through this world is actually a supernal learning experience designed to deliver us from the tyranny of fear this world offers.

Now that we have prepared ourselves for our thirty-day, self-paced Healing Virtues Retreat…let's begin!

Chapter Two

ATTITUDES, BELIEFS, AND VALUES

Your attitudes, beliefs, and values are at the very core of your essence and define the heart of what you do in this world and who you believe you are in the overall scheme of the cosmos.

- Introduction
- Arthur's Story
- Day One: God-Reliance
- Day Two: Humility
- Day Three: Acceptance
- Day Four: Mercy
- Day Five: Hope
- Attitudes, Beliefs, and Values Prayer

Introduction

Are you a body living in a physical world while striving for a spiritual reality, or are you a spiritual entity living in a physical world and required to heed the laws of the material realm? The answer to this question is the fulcrum upon which swings the balance of the meaning and purpose you give to your very existence. Your answer to this question is the foundation of the way you view life, the footing for all other attitudes and values you hold about virtually everything in your world. Your answer will tell you a great deal about your relationship with God and your attachment to the world. Without question, your answer will determine the degree to which your sickness will make you ill.

Noted Jesuit author John Powell defines attitudes as the lens through which you view your world the same way over and over again. Beliefs are strong emotional states of certainty that you hold about a specific person, thing, idea, or life experience. You have beliefs about virtually everything in the world. Your beliefs are like cow paths in your mind that you travel again and again. They form the basis for your personality, the fountainhead of your perceptions, the wellspring of your thinking, and the motivation for your actions. They determine what you value and what you don't, what assumptions you make, and the expectations you hold dear. In short, your attitudes, beliefs, and values are at the very core of your essence and define the heart of what you do in this world and who you believe you are in the overall scheme of the cosmos.

In order to develop and grow, to move through the maturation process, you are required to change. Change is the watchword of the universe, the only thing that does not change is change itself.

You cannot remain still; either you grow or you regress. In order to grow, you must change your attitudes from time to time. Smooth adjustment over the life span is a matter of attitudinal as well as behavioral modification. When growth knocks at your door in whatever disguise, it is your invitation for changing your attitudes. If you don't, you can't grow. This really isn't hard to understand. All you need do is remember the last time you were on a diet. If you were able during the diet to modify your attitudes about food and eating, then the progress you made could be sustained. If you were unsuccessful in changing your attitudes, you may have been able to squeeze off a few pounds, but they came back again within a very short time. For change to be lasting, you must modify your attitudes.

You are being challenged to grow right now in your life. Your sickness or physical malady hovers over you like an untamed giant. This monster can either destroy you or you can control it. You may have never thought of it this way, but your sickness is demanding that you change your attitudes.

What are the attitudes that require modification? You have a function in life that transcends the world you see, and you are being gently pulled toward that function. You have a Teacher inside you who quietly instructs you, speaks of peace, and offers another meaning and purpose for your sickness than the one the world offers. In order to really listen to your Teacher, you must change your attitudes. You can consult your inner Teacher any time through prayer. He will gently nudge you toward him and his healing power of love.

One aspect of love that spiritually awakening persons have learned well is gratitude. You can learn to replace attitudes that bring anger, malice, and revenge with attitudes that generate gratitude. Indeed, attitudes that generate bitterness in any form are poisonous to your emotional system.

Attitudes that bring bitterness are really illusions. They delude us into thinking our life is a merciless pursuit in which we are badgered ceaselessly and pushed about with cruel disinterest. Nothing could be further from the truth. You can replace such attitudes with this simple truth: Everything has a purpose if we can look past the worldly images of pain and invest ourselves in accurate thinking of God. This lesson is central for happiness, for modifying your illness into authenticity.

The lesson in gratitude is yours. If your eyes perceive without love, you perceive an empty shell and become blind and deaf to the Teacher within. The lesson of gratitude is mandatory for recognizing the abundance of God in all things and for abandoning the worldly belief in deprivation.

Your body must have a purpose, because it exists. Likewise, your sickness must also have a purpose, because it exists. Your body is a vehicle, a means of communication, a way to connect with other souls who have likewise been placed in bodies. Your body is a learning tool; it helps you facilitate a state in which the body becomes unnecessary on a higher plane than this earth. What, then, is the purpose of your sickness?

We are part of God's creation; therefore, because creation is whole and complete, we are likewise whole and complete. The mark of wholeness is holiness. Even though we are sinners, we are nonetheless, at our very depths, children of God and included in his complete universe no less than the birds and the trees, no less than the grass and the stars. We are of God, and he would not allow his children to suffer. Our bodies on the other hand are of this world and, therefore, can suffer. Our job is to separate our true self from our world self; a core lesson of sickness.

Whatever you truly believe in is what reality will be for you. In a sense, you create your own reality. For example, an attractive woman came to my office one day in great distress. Her husband had left her. As I inquired more deeply into her story, it became apparent that she believed her husband was perfect. As he was perfect in her eyes, she was imperfect. Indeed, without him she was nothing. It required several months of weekly sessions for her to grow enough so she could modify her attitudes of illusion into ones reflecting a more realistic distribution of worth in the relationship. I'm happy to report that this couple eventually did manage to construct a new relationship contract and find their way to new growth both personally and as a couple. It took a mammoth amount of work, however; their attitudes required massive modification.

Dr. Bernie Siegel reminds us that we may not have a notion of what wellness is all about. He challenges us to define it for ourselves, because what we believe wellness to be is the direction we will travel in our path away from sickness. He maintains that only about twenty percent of all patients even want to achieve total wellness. He maintains that some patients, perhaps fifteen percent, don't even want to live at all. A death wish buried in their unconscious all but sabotages any attempts to aspire to greater levels of wellness.

The rest of the patients, sixty to sixty-five percent, simply do as their doctors tell them, passively and without much interest or comment. These are the ones who really need care, because they are on the fence, so to speak, in their emotional and spiritual development. Where are you? Without the will to live, you cannot expect to surmount your current sickness. Without the will to love, you cannot hope to develop spiritually. Which group of these patients do you think will become spiritually awakening persons?

Norman Cousins echoed Siegel's ideas and underlined the role played by virtues in the drama we call life, especially when that life calls for us to deal with serious illness. In *Head First,* Cousins wrote:

Hope, faith, love, and a strong will to live offer no promise of immortality, only proof of our uniqueness as human beings and the opportunity to experience full growth even under the grimmest circumstances....Far more real than the ticking of time is the way we open up the minutes and invest them with meaning.

You have the power to change your very values, but it takes stamina, determination, and usually a dramatic stimulus. Your sickness can provide this stimulus if you accept it as a challenge and an opportunity rather than as a cruel punishment for a crime you are unaware of having committed. Your beliefs about what your sickness is and what it can be for you basically determine what your sickness will be. The choice is yours.

What is genuinely important to you? Your health? Your finances? Your longevity? Your family? Friends? Business or career?...What? The fundamental ethical, moral, and practical judgments we make about what's important will determine our values. When you are sick, you need all the awareness you can muster. You need to be alert, awake, and fully ready to learn the lessons of your illness — and learn them well. Who do you know who has learned the true value of living only after they became sick? What have you decided to believe in? Success or failure? Love or fear? Light or darkness? God or the world?

Anthony Robbins, author of the best-selling book *Unlimited Power: The Way to Peak Personal Achievement,* outlines the six beliefs he recognizes as necessary and sufficient for success in life. Now, keep in mind as you read these that they are not intended to be a Christian message. However, I would like you to apply them to what we have discussed thus far. I think you'll be surprised to realize how instructive these can be as we struggle with our broken bodies. Here are Mr. Robbins' six principles for peak personal achievement:

1. Everything happens for a reason and a purpose, and everything that happens serves us.
2. There is no such thing as failure. There are only results.
3. Whatever happens, take responsibility.
4. It's not necessary to understand everything to be able to use everything.
5. People are your greatest resource.
6. Work is play.

How can these six principles help you achieve peak performance during your time of sickness? Are they in keeping with the core ideas we have covered thus far? I think they are!

The Real You Your body is in the world and also of the world; it is, therefore, governed by the rules of the world. The real you — your genuine reality — is in this world but not of this world. The real you is governed not by the rules and laws of the material world like your body is but by the spiritual rules and laws of heaven. Your illness is of this world and can only affect that which is of this world. Your sickness cannot affect the real you. But the real you can learn and grow from the lessons your sickness teaches through your inner Teacher.

One of the attitudes that begs to be changed is the one that says we can experience misfortune. A replacement attitude that can serve as a beacon of hope is that all that confronts us in this world contains lessons we are to learn. Your sickness, then, contains lessons that your inner Teacher can help you learn. His will for you is to experience happiness, your inheritance as a child of God, and experience it undisturbed. This requires an immense modification of attitudes. We have always been taught that sickness held only bad for us. To adopt an attitude that sees some "good" coming from misfortune seems alien to our very being, and yet this is what we are called to do.

Arthur's Story

To look at this man, you would never guess that he had already lived ninety-one years. But Arthur was indeed born over ninety-one years ago on a small midwestern dirt farm. He was the only son of a father who had lost his left hand in a hunting accident at age twenty-six. Arthur remembers well how he would ride atop the cultivator behind the team of horses, pulling the reins to the right when his father, walking behind him, would yell "Gee!" and to the left when he heard the call "Haw!"

In 1920 Arthur's mother died, forcing his father to sell the old place "lock, stock, and barrel." Arthur moved to the big city to find work. He found more than work there. He married his wife, Ruth, and started a family shortly thereafter. In 1932, as the Great Depression gripped ever tighter, he lost his job. This turn of events sent him packing, with his growing family, back to his roots in the country.

In 1940 another tragedy struck. His twelve-year-old daughter was killed in a freak accident in the schoolyard. The next day, Ruth gave birth to their next child. "That's the way God works," says Arthur. "It's hard, but you have to keep on going." World War II came along, and Arthur's oldest boy found himself in the South Pacific with the Army. "The day I saw that letter from the Department of the Army with the black rim around it, I knew what it was. I cried for him and his mother. God knows what he's doing. I can't understand how he works, but I trust him."

Arthur says his health is excellent, and one would never suspect that this man has suffered through cancer and heart disease. He had a pacemaker implanted years ago and wears a hearing aid in each ear. He regularly goes turkey hunting with his sons and enjoys a healthy sense of humor; he's quick to flash a crackling smile. In 1952 he followed his father's footsteps, again selling the farm and returning to the city. Odd jobs and a rising faith sustained Arthur then and to this day. In 1984 Ruth was "taken home to God, which left me sad and alone for a while. My family is everything to me," says Arthur.

In 1923 Arthur came close to death in an auto accident. He recalls arriving at the doctor's office and then being taken to the hospital emergency room. "The doctors gave me up for dead," he says. "But two nurses came to me and turned me over on my stomach. I belched up a pint of blood. I felt much better immediately. I guess I would have died if they hadn't come over to me. That's a miracle, you know. Those nurses were actually angels. It wasn't my time yet, and I guess it still isn't."

Simple faith, acceptance, calm, childlike — all these terms describe Arthur. Arthur is absolutely positive in attitude. He embodies the adage that simplicity is beauty — and Arthur is beautiful.

Day One: God-reliance

To be God-reliant means to have unquestionable dependence on God's grace and power. To be God-reliant is to have confidence and absolute assurance in God, to place your full store of belief in him, to take stock of yourself as part of God. When you are God-reliant, your belief core is centered in God, and all you value is of God.

Doubt is the poison that invades God-reliance. It casts shadows of fear and insecurity on the reality of your sonship or daughtership with him. As you grow ever closer to God-reliance, you become more certain, convinced, secure, and calm. God is the indisputable and infallible center of your life.

In the light of God-reliance, your sickness becomes only a pesky reminder of your humanity and a mere bump along the road to strengthened conviction of God's guiding hand and certainty in the scheme of his plan.

᙮

Arthur exercises his God-reliance in many simple ways. For example, his reliance on God is evident in his relationship with the earth. "Where does oil come from?" questions Arthur. "God places it there, and as we need more, he'll make sure we'll have it."

Arthur's conviction that God is in charge is reflected in his attitude toward science. "Science is the study of learning how to use what God has put here for us. He's at work all the time." His assurance of God's omnipotence rests on solid beliefs. "Everything on this earth is valuable," he says. "God put it here for a reason. Things that we think are useless are simply the ones we haven't yet found how to use."

Arthur is practical and earthy in the most classic sense of the word. "God doesn't force anybody to do anything" says Arthur. "When you do the will of God, it's its own reward. It's a mystery to me," he confesses. "But there's no question that he's everywhere."

Meditations on God-reliance

MORNING

Today I am reborn in a new relationship.

This morning, I fully join in close relationship with God and accept this relationship as real, as my only true healing reality today. Through this relationship, I can place my full reliance on "the now" and abandon any hold on the past. Today I am reborn in a new relationship of wholeness, leaving all fragmented ones behind me.

AFTERNOON

I call for my release from illness.

Today I call for my release from illness and walk the path of wholeness. I release all from any grievances I hold against them so I will be released as well. I rely on God's grace to move me to the forgiveness necessary for release. As I perceive the healing of others, I likewise perceive my own healing as well and thus remember God all day long.

EVENING

Christ transcended this world through reliance on the Father.

As I close my eyes tonight, I am compelled in gladness to recall Christ's Resurrection, which strengthens my reliance on the Father because it is a symbol of joy for me. The Resurrection is Christ's triumph over the forces of the world. Christ transcended this world not by attack but through reliance on the Father. I, too, rely on him the whole night through and find deep delight in knowing he is with me always.

Day Two: Humility

Humility means being modest and unassuming. A humble person is poor in the sense of not requiring much to satisfy ego needs. Humility means being plain, clear, clean, and uncomplicated. Humility also means being free from worry and untainted by the cares of the world. It means being free from affectation and the need to play roles, take on an image, put on a mask, or put on airs. Humility means being honest with yourself and your fellow human beings, genuine, transparent. What a humble person shows on the outside is what's really on the inside. Humility means being simply, purely, solely, and even bluntly, you. It is truly knowing who you are: a child of God who is loved unconditionally.

୧ஃ

Arthur's humility is evident in much of what he professes. "My bad deeds would outweigh my good ones by a mile," he asserts. He recognizes his shortcomings clearly. "I'm not perfect. No, not by a long shot. I'm not too patient, you know. Things get to me sometimes." Yet there is no hint of guilt or vanity in his statements. They roll out of Arthur like gems of truth and plain facts of the matter. There's not the slightest hint of falsity about him, either. He is clear and uncomplicated, modest and straightforward.

His life is full of wonder. "How can a black cow eat green grass and give white milk?" questions Arthur with knowing awe. "Miracles happen every day, all the time."

Meditations on Humility

MORNING

Today the Holy Spirit calls me to see myself honestly.

Today I am humble, but my humility never asks that I remain content with littleness. Humility is God's honesty in action. Today the Holy Spirit calls me to see myself honestly. I am reawakened in the Holy Spirit with the promise "Seek and you shall find." Under guidance of the Holy Spirit, I cannot be defeated in humility.

AFTERNOON

What I appear to lose is simply another way to see God's light.

I know, in humble faith, that the Holy Spirit will never call upon me to sacrifice anything of celestial value. What I appear to lose is simply another way to see God's light and to develop new attitudes of love. Today I want to turn over the beliefs in my value system that bind me to the world and replace them with attitudes, values, and beliefs of another dimension — the one true dimension, which is peace. Healing is a part of my new belief system.

EVENING

My body cannot hinder my mind.

As the celestial night advances, I remind myself that my body cannot hinder my mind. I can transcend my body at will. Of itself, my body means nothing. My body is really outside the real me and can affect very little indeed. Tonight as I sleep, I will ask the Holy Spirit to transform my false beliefs about my body — that my body can give me peace. I now know that this is impossible.

Day Three: Acceptance

Acceptance is approving, honoring, and assenting. It's having a sense of being in accord with God, of being with God, in agreement with his will and in his grace. Acceptance is personally affirming. It enables us to adopt our true spiritual nature. It ratifies our essence. It allows us to feel in compliance with God, adhering to his truth, and willing to be one with him. It motivates us to give God and his reflections here on this earth our personal and heartfelt "amen." Acceptance acknowledges God's supremacy as our ultimate good and the source of our peace of mind. It gives us graciousness in heart and soul and allows us to reflect God's beauty outward. Acceptance substantiates us as children who are dependent upon God's freely given grace. It allows us to know that however noxious an experience may be, we can creatively accept his plan that love will eventually come of it.

ได

Arthur's acceptance of the love of God as the primary motivating force in his world takes many forms. He knows his physical maladies cannot really hurt him. He sees his age not with fear that the end is near but as God's grace and purposefulness in action. "If we didn't have love, we wouldn't have a country. We'd have war all the time, and people would only hate. If you have love, you have everything!" he exclaims with finality. "Look at the corn! Used to be you couldn't get more than fifty bushels from an acre. Now, with fertilizer, you can get one hundred fifty to two hundred bushels. And where did fertilizer come from? Why, from God of course."

Arthur focuses on God's gifts. He exudes truth, beauty, and goodness in a most childlike way. He knows that "the holy Power takes care of me. I've had so many close calls at work, in the fields, on the trains, everywhere. But God's angels take care of me. I know they do." Acceptance of God's overcare is simply part of who Arthur is.

Meditations on Acceptance

MORNING

Today I accept my real self.

I arise in total acceptance that there is no separation in me. Acceptance restores my wholeness of mind. I make a commitment to acceptance today, confident that my beliefs will be corrected where necessary. My acceptance of my real self will cancel out all errors and allow me to escape the fear that has descended upon me. Acceptance is gentle, since it's perfect accomplishment releases me from guilt. Today I accept my real self.

AFTERNOON

I accept myself and everyone as God's sons and daughters.

Acceptance is my healing device. I am made invulnerable as I accept truth. I am guaranteed safety and union as God's son or daughter through acceptance. I accept myself and everyone as God's sons and daughters. My final lesson is accepting the true reality of my existence. I am basically a spirit that is currently existing in my body but is encircuited directly to God.

EVENING

Acceptance gives me a healed mind.

As I accept at deeper and deeper levels, the inner light of healing is released to bathe my entire being with the power of Christ. Acceptance gives me the miracle of a healed mind, my attitudes are modified, my values are changed, and my beliefs are transformed. I can join in with the currents of Christ's love when I accept acceptance as a primary goal. Acceptance renders me guiltless and gives me peace. I welcome acceptance, preferring peace and integrity to pain and destruction — the lessons of the world.

Day Four: Mercy

Mercy goes far beyond the idea of pity. It encompasses leniency, forbearance, and most of all, compassion. Mercy means being humane and tender, empathic and full of grace. Mercy motivates us to be soft and feeling rather than severe and hardhearted. It allows us to touch and to sympathize rather than be pitiless and cruel. Mercy is humanitarian in the sense that Christ was compassionate to the sick. Mercy allows us to relent, to let go of judging and blaming, fault-finding and criticism. Mercy says "it doesn't matter"; let us simply give help and promote healing. Mercy grants clemency, it is interested in justice but first exercises pity and compassion.

Arthur exercises mercy most of all by living in peace. "I live by myself. I need to keep busy. I can't quit anything." Arthur is merciful to himself in seeing his care-needs clearly and feeling tenderness and empathy for his own desires. He refrains from self-judgment. He's not severe on his condition nor his human frailty. He can touch his own heart and open himself to God's grace. He extends his hands as would a child to receive rather than ridicule. He offers himself condolence, which brings solace and tender understanding. Arthur's way of living can make your heart melt and show you a way to graceful living.

Meditations on Mercy

MORNING

I am mercy itself.

Today I will let mercy ascend in my mind. My mind is aligned with God's universal mind in an attitude of mercy. Without my being aware of it, my beliefs may have been attacking my body all along. It's time to release the creative healing power of mercy, unleash the powerful potential of right belief and the soothing serenity of self-compassion. I am mercy itself.

AFTERNOON

My true reality is in the mind of God.

I deceived myself when I thought I was a body. My true reality is in the mind of God and radiates life and light from its source of mercy. That same source dwells in my center and is the fountainhead of healing waters that drives the rising tide of clarity, enabling me to change my mind about so many things. I am no longer a bobbing cork in a sea of turmoil. I know who I am. I am of God. I am of God's mind and know only God's mercy of healing.

EVENING

Mercy restores my awareness of healing.

The mercy I receive, I can also give. Mercy is at the center of the instants of release I offer myself. Mercy can reverse physical laws and replace them with God's laws. Mercy can roll back the consequences of sickness, allowing healing to emerge. Mercy restores my awareness of healing. It is the outward sign of inner healing. I praise God for mercy.

Day Five: Hope

Hope is our spiritual vehicle to bring confidence, assurance, and security into our hearts and minds. Hope is our constant reassurance that God is in charge and that we need not fear. Hope realizes the promise of fairness, goodness, and cheer. Hope enables us to keep our belief in the bright prospect of Christ's encouragement to us that his Spirit is with us always and that love will remain the compelling force in the world and beyond. Like the unwavering hope that sustained David when he went out onto the field to battle Goliath, hope gives us perfect expectation that God's will prevails and sustains us. Hope gives us spiritual optimism, full confidence, and bright enthusiasm, knowing that our fate is secure in God. Hope is the bright light of cheer that crowds out the darkness of despair, futility, and despondency.

る

Arthur's hope gleams through bright eyes that have learned much in his ninety-one years. "We know there are dishonest people who are only interested in money, but we also know there are righteous people who love their neighbor and don't try to take things from them." Hope for the world, hope for humanity, and absolute hope in God's loving power and ever-present care of his children is Arthur's simple message of living for us. "Deposits of ore are growing as we speak!" exclaims Arthur in vibrant testimony to his optimistic value system. "God's holy power takes care of me all the time." He doesn't need fear anymore because his hope is so vital, his presumption of God's love is so central, and his stability of character is so steadfast that he needs fear no longer. Fear is useless to him.

Meditations on Hope

MORNING

Today I choose hope.

Today I place my hope where certainty lies. In the past, I have placed hope where no hope can be, so naturally I have felt hopeless. Hope illuminates my mind, and I choose between a sleeping death with dreams of despair and a happy awakening with the joy of life. The abundance of hope is the natural result of choosing to follow Christ. Today I choose hope.

AFTERNOON

Now I am in the light of hope.

Now that I have found the light of hope, I realize the total inadequacy of my former attitudes, which chained me to the world. Have I been afraid to find hope in the past? Fear is no longer my leader; hope has replaced fear as my guiding light. Hope is my lantern in the darkness.

EVENING

I hear the whispers of hope nudging me to follow.

I accept the guidance of hope tonight. Hope is my guide; I depend on hope to bring me through the meaninglessness that sometimes overtakes me. As I follow this guide, any errors in belief or in former values will be corrected, opening the gates for healing to enter my life. Tonight as I go to sleep, I hear the whispers of hope nudging me to follow my inner Guide, who alone can carry me out of this earthly pit.

Attitudes, Beliefs, and Values Prayer

Let me merely close my eyes and forget all that I thought I knew and understood. Let me endeavor to relinquish every thought that clutters my mind and keeps me chained to this world. Let me give over every attitude, value, expectation, or assumption that blocks me from reason, sanity, and simple truth.

I am not a body. I am free, the same as God originally created me. Let me challenge all idle thoughts and exchange them for thoughts of God-reliance, humility, acceptance, mercy, and hope. Let me place myself in God's charge. Let me give myself over to the divine Physician, casting away my silly illusions, wishful thinking, and valueless attitudes. Let me understand clearly the values of peace, genuine healing, and forgiveness.

Let me become keenly aware of all the things I saved to settle for myself and thus kept away from God and my healing gift within. Let me give them over to the One who alone knows the mechanisms of healing, who knows the direction of healing, and who knows the substance of healing for me. Let me lean my head against his shoulder and rest awhile and find the peace within me. Let the ancient door to my soul swing free again, and let me listen to the echoes of love in my deepest memory. Amen.

Chapter Three

PERCEPTION

Our perceptions are as unique as our individual fingerprints. Everything we experience we see in our own way. Our "point of view" is truly our own.

- Introduction
- Sister Matthias' Story
- Day Six: Vision
- Day Seven: Humor
- Day Eight: Peace
- Day Nine: Adaptability
- Day Ten: Simplicity/Beauty
- Perception Prayer

Introduction

Events are what happen to us along the road of life. Many times we aren't even aware of the attitudes, beliefs, and values we hold in our innermost selves until we encounter an event that forces us to clarify exactly what we believe about the circumstances surrounding it.

Suppose you are walking down the street and see a robbery in progress. You are shocked and then begin to process this event in your mind. What should you do? So many values come into play here. Is this action wrong in your eyes? Does it "square" with your value system? Are you capable of doing anything about this event? Might you get hurt if you try to intercept the robber? Do you have a duty to do something, or should you pass on by without acting and hope someone else will make a move? Confusing questions like these swirl around in your mind as you grope for the "right" thing to do.

Perception of Events Perhaps the above example is a bit extreme. What about capital punishment or euthanasia or sexual harassment or living wills or a married priesthood? These value-laden subjects demand that we clarify our attitudes and beliefs if we are to achieve peace of mind. Such issues or events in our lives can be interpreted in various ways by different people; we certainly have differences of opinions in our culture. Before we can make judgments about these events, however, we must first perceive them. Our perceptions are as unique as our individual fingerprints. Everything we experience we see in our own way. Our "point of view" is truly our own. Let's take a look at perception.

An event is any factual happening in your life, be it an auto accident or a Thanksgiving dinner. An event can be a relationship such as the one you have with your auto mechanic or the intimacy you share with your spouse. An event can be a circumstance such as the fact that you have brown hair or live in Toledo or were born in 1939. Each of these events is a fact you will perceive in different ways.

An event in itself is quite neutral. It means nothing until you do something to it, that is, until you perceive it. Your perception of an event will align itself with the attitudes and values you have about the events and circumstances that surround it. The question for all of us as we advance in our spirituality is, how do we know when we are viewing the event in a "right" or holy perspective?

There is a way to look at any event in your life as simply another step toward God. You are called to view this world through the eyes of Christ. You can develop the perspective, or viewpoint, that all events are lessons God wants you to learn. You can constantly keep in mind that within this event is something you need to learn in order to take the next developmental step in your spiritual journey. In God, there are no contradictions.

How can you see your sickness as a lesson? Through your human eyes — your world-view — your sickness seems like a contradiction of the promise of a pleasant life, a disavowal of Christ's promise of abundance. In this view, you see your sickness as disharmony, as a trick that has been played on you, a bad dream, a betrayal of some covenant you have with God.

"God, why have you done this to me?" is a common lament from those who are suffering. Your disease is not an abandonment of divine grace or a punishment of insane proportion. It is not an attack on your integrity or a violation of your very being. What, then, is it? How can you begin to see your disease as a lesson — and, indeed, as a lesson in what? How can you change the perception of your sickness so as to transform it from a tragedy into a holy event which can let the light of heaven shine in?

Forgiveness Forgiveness brings peace, and peace begins when you can perceive your world as being different than it was before. Peace is the bridge you can walk to leave this world behind. There is no peace except that which comes from God. God is sure, and even though you may feel he has abandoned you, that is impossible. You are now being called to change your very perspective on healing.

When you pray to God for healing, what do you mean and what does God hear? So many times our perception of healing involves things of this world. God's perception of healing involves only things of heaven and the Spirit. The world deceives us. It tells us to view our body as ourselves. To bring order to conflicting goals, senseless journeys, vain pursuits, and meaningless endeavors, you must learn to see yourself and this world differently. You are not your body, and this world is only your temporary home.

The world sees things — all things — as separate and distinct. God sees things as whole, not separate. We engage in partial vision. We see things as through a knothole in a fence, seeing only what is available to us to see, but we make assumptions about the entirety as though we could see the whole. You see your sickness as separate and distinct. How can you change this and see your disease as part of a whole, part of something that makes sense?

If your perception stops where the world perceives things, then it stops short of giving you true meaning. Your sickness can only have meaning and purpose when you can view it as being a part of the larger whole of your life. Even though your disease is in and of this world, the Holy Spirit can transform what seems to have no meaning into something that has an abundance of meaning if you will only let him into your life and open to the healing power within you.

Only forgiveness can release you from the false perception that your body is your home. Only forgiveness can persuade you to recognize your own holiness, seen as wholeness. You can be one with the spiritual healing power within you. Once you have given yourself the gift of true sight, then the pain of fear will be lifted from you.

Shift Your Perspective Your sickness may be shifting your perception of your body from one misperception to another. Before your disease, you may have viewed your body as the source of all earthly pleasure. If so, it maintained the central focus of your life as you pursued bodily comfort and pleasure. Now, after the diagnosis of your illness, you may have shifted to another equally misguided perspective of your body, seeing it now as the source of evil for you, the core of all anguish, the seat of fear, and the source of attack. You must grow to view your body simply as a teaching aid, no matter what physical condition it may be in right now.

Only God can give you the means by which your perception is made true, beautiful, and accurate. You must learn to see blessing, not attack, in all things, even illness. You need to learn to give as much consistent effort as you can to seeing the future as belonging to God and concentrating on the present. Learning the earthly lesson of giving God power over your illness allows you the grand opportunity to tap into your ultimate healing power.

When you look at your illness with human eyes, there is nothing to see except misery and pain, bitter disappointments, bleak despair, hopelessness, and doubt. Yet when you look through the eyes of Christ, the beautiful sight you can see is peace of mind. Open your eyes, then, and see that heaven lies before you and within you through a door marked *forgiveness,* which leads to peace. But you must change your mind about the purpose of the world. You will be bound until you see all as blessed; blessed in the sense that it offers you the opportunity to see who you really are and to exercise testimony to that reality.

According to Dr. Bernie Siegel, we misperceive where healing comes from when we give credit to the disease, rather than to the person who was afflicted, when healing takes place. He says that the medical community usually attributes a "miraculous" cure to a "slow-growing tumor" or a "well-behaved cancer" or perhaps an "error in diagnosis." Yet none of these things fully explains many healings he has seen right in his own office.

Dr. Siegel also believes that sickness is often a sign that some kind of change is needed in the person's life. Again, it's all in the way we look at it. Norman Cousins says much the same thing when he writes: "Diseases are classifiable, to be sure, but most of the patients who had them are not….[But] the need of the physician to motivate or inspire patients remains constant."

Reframing Anthony Robbins defines a process he calls *reframing*. By reframing, he simply means seeing an event in a different context than you previously had. For example, the sound of footsteps in your kitchen at night when you are in bed has a completely different meaning from footsteps you hear while walking along a sidewalk in broad daylight on a busy street. What is the difference between the following two women who each stayed a weekend at the same elegant hotel? One described her visit as "miserable." "Saturday night our waiter scowled at the maître d' all evening," said the first woman. The second woman described her stay as "marvelous." She playfully reported, "There was even a little intrigue going on between our waiter and the maître d' on Saturday night." Both women experienced the same hotel, the same service, food, and amenities. Yet each came away with opposite opinions, because each framed the experience differently. Each woman was coming from a completely separate point of view.

Your task is to reframe the illness that has afflicted your body. Three days before his death, John Adams, the second president of the United States, wrote the following, using a house as a metaphor for his body:

> The house in which John Adams lives is falling down. The roof leaks badly. The foundation is crumbling. The shingles are dropping like raindrops, and the windows let the frigid air through like screens. In spite of all this, however, John Adams is doing just fine, thank you.

John Adams' spirit of resiliency and steadfast character is like the perception Christ gave to his children as he hung on the cross and lamented "Father, forgive them for they know not what they do" (Luke 23:34).

Spiritual Sight We are all called to develop "spiritual sight." Where we have such faith, we no longer deny what we cannot see with our physical eyes. We need to rearrange our perspective and understand that there are different kinds of sight, each requiring its true level. When we confuse levels of perception, we can get sick. We need to make our perceptions holy — to make them whole. We need to perceive all with love, because if we neglect to focus with love, we see only empty shells and fail to see the truth in what confronts us.

Sister Matthias' Story

Sister Matthias Haberberger, a Sister of Mercy, wrote the following personal account about six months after the termination of her chemotherapy. Today she is very much alive and well, practicing God's work in her life and awakening to even greater heights of spiritual awareness.

"It seems that in times of crisis, such as illness, the Lord reveals himself and gives special graces to you so that you can accept whatever may happen in ways he ordinarily does not. Perhaps it is also a means to help me understand better who he is and what he is all about. I think this is what has happened to me. I am grateful and I thank and praise God.

"In October 1977, I experienced a slight pain in my left side and lower abdomen plus some hemorrhaging. I didn't go to see my family doctor because my next regularly scheduled appointment in early December seemed soon enough. In November, the pain became more severe, but I still didn't see the doctor.

"When December finally did roll around, I saw him and described my symptoms. He shook his head, saying, 'You are much too young for something like this.' I began to wonder what he meant. He immediately referred me to another doctor, whom I saw a few days later. Before I left home that morning, I spent some time in prayer, and this is the first time I prayed like this. I said, 'Lord, I don't know what to expect when I see this doctor today, but whatever it is, I'm ready and I surrender myself to you.'

"I never did return home that day! After the examination, the doctor phoned St. John's Mercy Medical Center to arrange for a D and C that afternoon. When I called for the results a few days later, I said, 'Doctor, I know what you are going to tell me.' He said, 'Yes…you have cancer. I am turning you over to Dr. Blythe. He is one of the best oncologists. He will do the surgery.' Strangely, I was not alarmed or frightened about this news. I felt the presence of God and that he had touched my life in a way I had never been touched before. I believe that my prayer and what the doctor said had prepared me.

"After a week of various tests, Dr. Blythe performed a hysterectomy, which was quite successful. I felt the nearness of God during this time. I felt that Jesus was ministering to me in the doctors and nurses. I felt totally and completely in God's hands. I was not afraid. In Mark's Gospel (1:40-45), we read that Jesus cures a leper but gives a stern warning not to tell anyone. However, the man is so happy that he runs and tells everyone about Jesus. That's how I felt. I wanted to tell everyone what Jesus was doing in my life. I felt that the cancer was a grace.

"Dr. Blythe felt sure he had removed all the cancer, but a week later he started chemotherapy treatment as a precautionary measure. I was to undergo a series of five daily treatments once a month for six months. During this time, I began to read Scripture, which opened me up; it seemed as if the words spoke directly to me in a more meaningful way than ever before. The chemotherapy was administered into my veins through an IV on the top of my hand. This was done for five consecutive evenings, Sunday through Thursday for six months.

"On Sunday evening I received two drugs. The first was the 'real killer' in that it stung so much as it was administered and caused the most severe side effects. The other four evenings I received only one drug, with the exception of the last series of treatments.

"When the drug went into my veins, I felt a painful burning sensation. At this time my thoughts centered on Jesus. I imagined what pain he must have felt when the nails were driven through his hands and feet. He suffered all that because he loves me. Keeping my eyes fixed on Jesus helped me get through those treatments.

"There were times however, at the beginning, when I became somewhat discouraged and wanted to discontinue the treatment because it was so uncomfortable. In fact, during the second series I asked the doctor if it was absolutely necessary for me to take the six series of treatments. He assured me that I did in fact need to take the thirty (five times six) treatments for it to be effective.

"Needless to say, I asked myself, 'Why? Why did this happen to me?'

One day I was reading the following Scripture passage, which I saw as very affirming, 'As [Jesus] passed by he saw a man blind from birth. His disciples asked him, "Rabbi, who sinned, this man or his parents, that he was born blind?" Jesus answered, reassuringly, "Neither he nor his parents sinned; it is so that the works of God might be made visible through him' " (John 9:1-3). This touched me. God was using my cancer to show his work in my life.

"In April, I was due back at the hospital for my fourth series of treatments. At home I had regained my appetite, put on some weight, and was feeling much better. But I was very apprehensive about going back for another treatment. On that Sunday morning, I was again in prayer. Something happened! I know the Lord spoke to me. He said something like 'You have my healing power within you.' With tears in my eyes, I said, 'Lord, could you maybe just inhibit those bad effects of the chemotherapy when I go back to the hospital this afternoon?' With that request, I felt strengthened. I was ready to go, and I knew things would be different this time.

That evening, before my first treatment, a priest came into my room. He prayed with me and anointed me. The physical aftereffects of the previous treatments had included a number of losses: loss of appetite, loss of weight, and loss of hair. The only thing I seemed to gain was nausea, and certainly I never wanted that. However, except for the first treatment, none of these effects occurred during this series of treatments.

"I understand that a stronger drug was administered that first night. I believe that after some time one's body begins to tolerate the drugs better, but I also believe in the power of prayer and healing. I began to see the chemotherapy not as a drug but as the Lord's healing going through my bloodstream healing me. It was at this time that I felt the Lord calling me to a new ministry; to someday witness to what he was doing in my life, to be able to help others in some type of prayer or healing ministry. How this might be accomplished was not clear.

"During my final series of treatments in July, three or four different types of drugs were administered. I experienced aftereffects during the first two treatments. So I began to pray in a similar manner as described earlier. The final three treatments carried no ill effects whatsoever! I feel certain that the Lord was there with me, that he intervened and healed me; otherwise, I may not have finished the thirty treatments at all. I know that nothing can be attributed to anything that I may have done. It has been God's gift, for which I am most grateful."

Day Six: Vision

To have vision means to see the world as through the eyes of Christ. With vision, everywhere we gaze we see the beauty, the truth, and the goodness of God in action. Vision is the mystical awareness that something beyond this world lies just outside the confines of the material level. As we develop more and more vision, we can see the light of Jesus shining just behind the physical form of everyone and everything we observe.

To have vision is to distinguish between those things that are God's and those that belong to the world. When Christ said, "Render to God what is God's and to Caesar that which is Caesar's," he was speaking to our ability to recognize the difference between the two. Christian vision implies introspection and the ability to contemplate life and behold the specialness of everything in it from the point of view of Christ.

Vision allows us to catch a glimpse of heaven here on earth. It enables us to open our eyes and discern the gloriousness of our lovely and charming existence. Vision allows us the unusual and farsighted perspective that all is well, a viewpoint that the world is good. The opposite of vision is blindness, the inability to see the spiritual level of our true reality.

During her treatment for cancer, Sister Matthias was transformed by the virtue of vision. She was able to see beyond the IVs and the injections, to see through the starkness of the physical form of her therapy to an entirely different reality that lay just behind the busyness of the medical community in action. She imagined her drugs as light from Christ, the nurses and doctors as ministers of Christ's mercy, and the surgery as the gentle pulling and tugging of the power of God in the hands of human beings. Everywhere she placed her gaze, she became exquisitely aware of the work of God on this earthly plane.

Sister was able to seize the specialness of her condition and immediately discern that here was an opportunity for learning God's ways even more deeply than she had done previously. She saw Jesus in the priest who anointed her; she viewed her chemotherapy as God's healing impulses rushing through her bloodstream like diamonds in the night sky, healing and energizing her. She actually developed a new point of view that enabled her to see her cancer as a blessing and a grace, not something to be feared.

Sister Matthias' learning experiences during her cancer remain with her today. She says, "My illness helped me because I began to see in a new and different way. I believe the Lord intervened. I now think that Jesus and I are one because he lives within me. My perception is that Jesus is my healer in a very real sense and that I share in that healing power because he lives within me. My sickness has brought me into a personal relationship with Jesus. I now see so clearly who Jesus is and who I am. Jesus is alive and real."

Meditations on Vision

MORNING

The vision of Christ resides in me.

As I awaken from darkness, I can see the radiance of God's guiltless Son. The vision of Christ resides in me, so I can see myself all day as the Holy Spirit sees me. Abba, allow your vision to correct my worldly perception and lift me beyond the hallucinations of my fear. Today is a day of healing; let me see how healing abounds in me every minute.

AFTERNOON

All is healed when seen with vision.

As the day extends, Lord, allow your vision to extend my own so I can attach my faith and perception to you. Let me see the vision of your love in everything today. Fear is but a delusion. I needn't be frightened by anything, knowing that all is healed when seen with vision. Today let me look past this earth to glimpse the soft light of heaven just beyond the form of this world.

EVENING

My spiritual sight penetrates all.

As night comes, let me remember that what I formerly perceived as obstacles are not so at all. Vision allows me to see through the darkness and look past this sometimes senseless world. Vision shows me the way tonight and every night. My spiritual sight penetrates all and illuminates the truth, beauty, and goodness of the healing that is happening even as I pray this prayer. I am blessed to see all the newness in you.

Day Seven: Humor

Humor is the faculty of discovering, expressing, or appreciating the ludicrous or absurdly incongruous. Humor allows us to find the world and our quirks and actions amusing. Humor demands that we view ourselves objectively. We must stand back from ourselves in order to see the levity in what we do. Persons with a good sense of humor are quick to recognize the light side, the bright side — even the inspiring side — of the human condition in almost any situation.

Humor also implies joy. To express joy is to find great delight, exultation, revelry, and jubilation in the knowledge that God is here. Joy urges us on; it encourages us to retain a disposition of gaiety, a mood of gladness, a lively wit, and a playful peace of mind. Humor is welcoming and hospitable, optimistic and sparkling; it gives contentment and offers serenity. Humor allows us to laugh and be glad. Christ instructed us to find cheer and be glad as a means of comforting us, to give hope and encouragement in a world which seems to offer only discontentment and lamentation.

❧

Sister Matthias was not frightened when she was diagnosed with cancer. Instead, she immediately felt that God had touched her in a unique way. She expressed humor in her ability to turn away from the potential horror and overwhelming seriousness of her condition and stand objectively in God's lightheartedness. She could step back and understand her illness in a completely different way.

In a sense, she delighted in her condition, not because of the pity she received from others but because she experienced the joy of knowing firsthand the healing power of God. She was motivated to be optimistic and cheerful. She experienced the promise of God in her life as she had never felt it before.

Sister Matthias was given the grace through humor to maintain a positive attitude and a supernal gratitude throughout her malady. Today she is delighted to be a better person, Christian, and child of God because of her sickness. She shows no trace whatsoever of her cancer; it seems to have disappeared. She discovered that even in the depths of grave sickness there is cause for joy and laughter instead of dread and depression. She concluded, "God makes all things work together for good for those who love him. God brings good out of everything!" How could anyone not be full of humor who can grasp the genuine meaning of this statement as Sister Matthias can?

Meditations on Humor

MORNING

My sickness allows me to learn what I need to know.

Let me awaken with a smile on my face to find you with me still, my divine Friend. My sickness is but a temporary way that allows me to learn what I need to know. I can find humor in the awkward seriousness I attached to my disease before I knew the value it offered to me. I smile broadly as your healing strength tickles my soul with lightness and mirth.

AFTERNOON

I revel in the laughter I hear in my soul.

Beyond the gray skies, the sun shines and I'm happy. I revel in the laughter I hear in my soul, knowing I'm no longer frightened. Your grace lets me dance inside, shedding any sourness that may have grown there. I'm simply filled with the bright side of reality as I see the gaiety of your wishes for me.

EVENING

My face brightens as I perceive your plan for my wellness.

The night is welcoming and hospitable as the serenity of gladness rests gently in me. I'm filled with the action of healing wit and soothing joy this evening as I contemplate the joy you bring. Let me smile as I sleep with the omnipotent power of your wholeness. My face brightens as I perceive your plan for my wellness.

Day Eight: Peace

Peace is a state of tranquillity in which we can recognize the great quiet and celestial security that is our inheritance from God. To be at peace is to be free from disquieting thoughts or emotions. Peace means to experience the supreme silence that is heaven within. Certainly, peace means living in amity and friendship. It implies harmony and concord in a world that seems bent on contention and attack. Peace is only from God. The world cannot offer peace, because peace is not from the world. The world cannot give what it doesn't possess. Only God gives peace, because it is the product of love.

Peace can reside and even grow in a mind that is able to accept God's plan for happiness and live it each day. Peace is the virtuous product of recognizing that our only goal is peace of mind and that our only gift to our brothers and sisters is peace itself. Peace is the state where love abides and seeks to share itself. Peace of mind is a requisite for truly understanding our relationship with God. Peace is always inside of us. We cannot disturb it; we can only obscure it with clouds of fear, guilt, and doubt. Healing is offered to those at peace. Our peace is limitless when we know God. The still infinity of endless peace surrounds us and embraces us always.

Sister Matthias reports that during the time of her surgery and treatment, she was captured by God's comforting presence in a way she had never been before. "I felt spiritually possessed. I'm sure it was a special grace given to me so I could grow through my illness. With that presence came a sense of profound peace, a strange belief that I had been chosen, a deep security that God's invisible hand was at work in me. I experienced a peace knowing that all was right with God, that everything was in control and in his hands. I felt sure that he was right there with me."

Since her illness, Sister enjoys a deeper peace than ever before, and she holds a conscious conviction that nothing from the outside world can disturb this peace. "I could hide myself from God and lose my peace, but that's not likely to happen. I want to be with God and have God be with me. That's why I know God will never fail to provide me with peace — it's impossible."

Her Bible has become her daily companion. "In it, Jesus says that peace is his farewell gift. I have become aware that God's will for me is peace of mind. I come to this peace by focusing on him, not on circumstances."

Meditations on Peace

MORNING

I make way for your peace, Lord.

I rise to find that I abide in peace where God would have me be. Allow me, divine Healer, to permit your peace to enter my soul so I can bring peace into my world. I make way for your peace, Lord. Let me not stand in its path or obscure it in any way. Let me be the instrument of my own peace and not the obstacle. My eyes see only peace. Your limitless, peaceful presence blesses the very place I lay my head this morning.

AFTERNOON

I embrace your peace and see it penetrate my depths.

Let your peace, Lord, settle upon the battleground of my sickness. Let the peace that lies deep inside me expand and flow through every pore and bathe each cell of my body, extending your reach to my very innards. I embrace your peace and see it penetrate my depths. Allow me to forgive all I need to so peace can fill the vacuum where my grievances formerly resided.

EVENING

You teach me peace all night through.

How lovely your peaceful healing feels, Lord. I extend your peace as I dream this night of your lush garden of love, which bears healing fruits I need only pick and eat, tasting the sweetness of your holiness. I lay down my head tonight in perfect peace, understanding that I need do nothing to merit your generosity; your outpouring of peace continues without end. I need only accept it as gift, completely awake as I sleep to the healing power of grace. You teach me peace all night through.

Day Nine: Adaptability

To be adaptable is to adjust to the surrounding conditions so as to survive in the most agreeable manner. To be adaptable is to conform, to adopt another's ways as our own.

Christian adaptability means to take on the ways of Christ. It means to conform to his precepts and wishes, to adopt his will. Adaptability means we must put aside the things of this world — the things that we might falsely hold dear — and take up those things that are of God. To be adaptable is to convert from the bleakness of the world to the brilliance of heaven. Persons who are adaptable work each day to make themselves agreeable to God. They endeavor to bring themselves in correspondence with him and to harmonize themselves with heaven. To be adaptable is to accommodate our needs to God's, to reconcile ourselves to the will of the Father.

Sister Matthias was blessed early in her bout with cancer, both in her knowledge of God's nearness and in her profound alignment with his will for her. She was able to surrender her will to his without struggle. She could only have achieved this surrender so thoroughly and so quickly through grace. This grace was extended to a person who had already tilled her spiritual soil in a most patient and loving way. She was able to adapt to whatever the Lord would have her do. She allowed him to take the reins of her life completely.

Sister Matthias strongly believes that people are not to blame for their own illness. "He never gives me more than I can endure," she says. She believes implicitly that "everything happens for a purpose and in God's time. Jesus doesn't see evil; he sees only truth, beauty, and goodness." Sister is staunch in her belief that prayer, in faith and trust, is the root of all healing. Prayer allows us to participate in the healing process and to maximize the medical treatment we receive. "I have learned that in my own weakness and my helplessness lies my real strength — my strength in God."

Meditations on Adaptability

MORNING

Teach me today that I can change.

Holy Friend, teach me today that I can change. I can adjust my perceptions and fearful beliefs, transforming them into love. Let me fix my purpose today upon your cause, which is only love. I see your mighty force of love, able to move anything. Let me grasp my function, Lord. What I formerly did not understand is now clear. I can change my gaze and make all things real — eternal.

AFTERNOON

I adapt my will to yours, Lord.

God, grant me the gift of adapting to your will. By adapting, I am finally embracing what has been changeless all along. What appeared to be real, I see now as mere illusion. Healing is happening within me. I am no longer separated from you, Lord, because I adapt my will to yours. Today I am as flexible as a palm tree swaying gently in the breeze. I resist nothing from God. I am open and accepting of all healing and love from you.

EVENING

Now I am free to change my view.

My healing proceeds according to your divine laws. I tear down the last encumbrances I had constructed to keep you away. Now I am free to change my view away from the earthly power of sickness to the healing power of love. My healing is producing harmony in me now as I retire from the day and rest in your quiet, delighted that you have given me the grace to change my point of view. I adapt my being to your will, O Lord, tonight.

Day Ten: Simplicity/Beauty

Simplicity and beauty are two separate concepts, yet they overlap to create a new concept we may call "simply beautiful" or "beautifully simple." Since these terms still fail to capture the full meaning of the two concepts in one, I decided to retain the term *simplicity/beauty.*

Simplicity is the state of being uncomplicated, innocent, without pretense. Simpleness is clarity. It is pure, basic, direct, straightforward, completely open, and understandable. Beauty brings pleasure to or exalts the mind or spirit. Beauty is loveliness, gracefulness, charm, and attractiveness. Beauty is brilliant, magnificent, and radiant.

The combination of these two qualities — simplicity and beauty — creates a virtue wherein one is exquisitely childlike in innocence and simply naive in openness and candor. Mary expressed the virtue of simplicity/beauty when she accepted the message from the archangel Gabriel. She was totally trusting, simply stunning, and magnificent in her willingness to surrender to the will of God, although she must have known the complications it would create. She was pure and clean, delicate, elegant, glorious, and radiant.

Sister Matthias reminds us that we must "turn and become like children" if we hope to enter the kingdom of heaven. (See Matthew 18:3.) She presents us with a picture of a patient quite different from the one Dr. Bernie Siegel paints as his "exceptional patients." Exceptional patients are so participatory that they may interfere with, even obstruct, doctors and nurses from performing what they need to do. Though they may participate in their own treatment in ways that give their bodies "live" messages, they can become trying for some members of the medical community at times.

Sister Matthias, on the other hand, seems to accomplish the same task of participatory partnership with her medical specialists but in a very different way. Instead of demanding, she accepts. Instead of critical questioning, she blesses. Instead of controlling, she adapts. And instead of creating complications and complexities, as some exceptional patients tend to do, Sister Matthias exercises simplicity and beauty. I am not proposing that such a posture as a patient is best for everyone. Different persons need to assume different ways of relating to their medical specialists. This, however, was Sister Matthias' way, and it appears to have succeeded well for her.

Meditations on Simplicity/Beauty

MORNING

Your beautiful healing honors my soul.

I open my eyes to your work, divine Physician. I see now that the body cannot heal; it is only your beautiful mercy that honors my soul with its healing potential. I dedicate my sight to the eternal and see the celestial beauty of your healing descending upon me and resting gently there all day.

AFTERNOON

I am transformed.

Today I needn't question the simple beauty of the grace that transcends all understanding. I perceive my joy through the vision of your healing work within me. I see the purpose of my sickness. Its beauty startles me, but I feel no sorrow, only the beauty of joy. Your simple love allows me to see the same in me, and I am transformed.

EVENING

Love's healing sparkles through me.

Tonight I rest in the beautiful perception that I am one with you, dear Friend. Healing is in your mind, and therefore in mine as well. I see through the eyes of Christ as I dream of the light of healing seeping into each part of me. I feel the beautiful brightness of love's healing sparkling through my veins, bringing the silence of the universe into me.

Perception Prayer

Let us join our minds as we sit in silence and repeat God's name, along with the names of our brothers and sisters. Within our quiet minds, we have established an altar that allows us to reach God. Repeat God's name and all the tiny, senseless things of this world slip into true and rightful perspective. Repeat God's name and see how quickly you forget those things you formerly valued but that you now realize have no meaning. Be gentle with yourself, for you have done no wrong. You have simply grown beyond the valueless into a new order that you found in the silence of your soul. God can hear only requests that are in harmony with divine laws.

Let us listen and be open to the healing power within. Let us invite the Holy Spirit to illuminate our sight and transform our perceptions into vision. Let us see through the eyes of Christ. Let us call upon God's name and recognize that we touch the healing power within. Lord, help us to bring healing to our perception so we may see all things through the eyes of Christ. My condemnation and my lack of forgiveness keeps my vision dark, and through my sightless eyes I cannot see the vision of my glory. Yet today I can behold this glory and be glad. Remind me now, Abba, for I am weary of the world I see. Reveal what you would have me see instead. Amen.

Chapter Four

THINKING

It is your conscious thoughts that give you the power, or lack of it, to exercise control over the events in your life and, more importantly, over the way you respond to those events.

- Introduction
- Gheil's Story
- Day Eleven: Faith
- Day Twelve: Wisdom
- Day Thirteen: Love
- Day Fourteen: Wholeness
- Day Fifteen: Charity
- Thought Prayer

Introduction

Thoughts are our internal communications to ourselves — what we say to ourselves. What we eventually decide to do in our lives is determined first by our thoughts. In most instances, we don't lack the necessary resources to achieve our goals; we lack control over these resources. The same is true for the way we think about our illness. What do you say to yourself about your illness? What are your thoughts? And what resources for coping can you control so you can use your illness to grow beyond the physical dimensions your sickness presents you?

It is your conscious thoughts that give you the power, or lack of it, to exercise control over the events in your life and, more importantly, over the way you respond to those events. Your thoughts can represent the lower or bodily level of experience or the higher or spiritual level of your experience. Which self is in control in your life — in control of you? To which do you give your trust?

In transcending sickness, your task is gradually to place your mind in the service of the Holy Spirit, the true source of healing within you. Indeed, your mind can elect to serve God or the world. If you wish to transform your thinking from focus on fear to focus on love, then you must look inside and change your mind. To change your mind means to place it at the disposal of true authority, that power that finds its source in heaven.

Our myopic and critical focus on the world, as well as our apparent denial of what lies beyond it, is what makes the world seem so real to us. In this way, we ensure that our thoughts will be full of misery and death rather than life and living. The thought of God is in us; it made us. Therefore, it can never leave us. God's thought is our true reality. God's thought in us is our source of life; we can tap this thought whenever we want. Eternity shines within us and offers only what is our inheritance as children of God: joy, peace of mind, and healing. Can you sense the thoughts of God within you? How can you get closer to understanding what God's thought means for you?

Train your mind to lay aside denial and accept the thought of God as your true inheritance. Christ's power is in your mind. No deprivation or pain can ever cut you off from God's sustaining love.

We are called to change our minds about the purpose of the world and the meaning of our bodies. When we move beyond the thoughts the world teaches — dismay, dismemberment, disharmony, and disunity — we come to recognize that all is blessed. It is at this point of enlightenment that we can grasp the thought of God within us and find peace. Peace of mind is our central goal in life.

The Wisdom of the Body Dr. Siegel believes that there is an internal wisdom of the body. The body somehow knows, he states, the natural course of healing and how to get there. We need to heed these body messages because they contain the "loving intelligence of the universe." When we listen within, the voice is saying, "Here is your path," and our symptoms call our attention back to this true path. Likewise, Norman Cousins reminds us that an overreliance on the technology of medicine can make us discount such important skills of medicine as "greater attention to communication needs, awareness of the importance of reassurance, increased emphasis on the need to understand the circumstances of a patient's life and not just his (her) symptoms."

Changing Our Minds We need to train our minds to think the thoughts of Christ. Our function is to live in this world and deal with it confidently, while learning always to transcend it. We need to relinquish everything that clutters our minds. Permit no thought to go unchallenged. Whenever you find your mind invaded by thoughts that disturb you, recognize that you have the power to rid yourself of these unwanted invaders. Simply say to yourself, "This thought I don't want. Instead, I choose to think _____." Allow Christ's thoughts to become your own. This can happen when you call upon the Father's name in faith and wisdom and love and wholeness and charity.

What are the thoughts that rule your mind? Do they force you to grope through the darkness, using your reason only to justify your criticism and your attack? Our understanding is so cluttered that what we think we understand is often but confusion born of stress. We are lost, and many times we worship what is really not there. We need to learn to place the future in the hands of God, to shift our thinking and become as accurate as possible.

Your Body Your body has let you down. Was there ever a question, a doubt, that it was destined to do just that? It is the mandate, the natural law, of all things physical to fall apart, to lose their internal organization. It is only when our minds no longer see themselves as our bodies that accurate thinking prevails. When accurate thinking commands our minds, fear cannot enter in and the mind attaches itself to the true reality, love.

The Holy Spirit is the home of minds that seek freedom. You are not bound to be helpless and afraid within your body. You are not a captive of the bag of bones you have carried around with you on your earthly journey. You are not a slave.

Judgment We need to get out of the judgment business. A thought cannot be neutral; either it is an evaluation, a judgment that speaks of condemnation, or it is a statement of learning, harmony, and a recognition of love in action that therefore speaks of forgiveness. There is no middle ground.

When we have an unforgiving thought, we make a judgment we do not doubt, even though the thought is not true. An unforgiving thought frantically twists and overturns all reason. With distortion as its purpose, the unforgiving thought attempts to superimpose worldly laws onto the laws of the universe. It tricks us into believing that our own condemnation is actually a law of its own, so we go around seeking allies in our quest to make our own deceptive condemnation real. Forgiveness, on the other hand, cannot judge and teaches us to welcome truth exactly as it is.

God's promise, and the purpose of Christ's earthly sojourn, is to replace our thoughts of conflict and fear with thoughts of peace. Such a process could only be accomplished through forgiveness, the basis for healing. There is always a need for healing whenever the mind is split. We need to recognize that our minds are but fragments of the one Mind, which has the sole power to heal. Likewise, we should not forget that our thoughts of separation, our dreams of malice, and our misperceptions all serve to hide the altar to the holy name of God within us.

Gheil's Story

In March 1990, after having smoked three packs of cigarettes a day for thirty years, Gil Griffin was informed by his physician that he had terminal lung cancer and had approximately four months of physical life left. Gheil, as he is known to his friends, was forty-six years old at the time. The father of three children, he had been divorced for eighteen years. A harder worker the world had seldom seen.

He had traveled extensively on business and was now about to begin a journey the likes of which he had never experienced before.

Even today, after he has not only survived but grown in ways he could not have imagined previously, Gheil still finds it difficult to describe his thoughts when he heard his physician's pronouncement. In faith, he began immediately to search for his unique gift of the Spirit, that individual purpose in life he had not recognized before. At first, he didn't have a clue how to embark on this search. He only knew that for him it was mandatory. Now that he can look back on the process, which at that time was a journey taken in blind faith, he can discern that order and direction were miraculously given to that journey by the Spirit.

The first step for Gheil was to praise God fervently, to solemnly praise his "sweet name" ten to twelve times an hour. Gheil relates that he did this for three to four days following his diagnosis. "Jesus Christ was on my mind every waking hour of the day," he exclaims.

The second step proceeded naturally from the first as Gheil began several days of simply offering thanksgiving to God. He gave profound thanks for everything he saw, experienced, or remembered. Gheil could see his life in a completely new way; there was no trace of judgment, anger, resentment, or sorrow. He was consumed, permeated, drenched in thanks for what God had given to him.

The third step consisted, relates Gheil, of praying out loud. He says that this sometimes caused raised eyebrows when the nurses came to check on him as he lay in his hospital bed. He would simply close his eyes and continue to pray out loud, always keeping his train of thought focused on Jesus. This lasted for another three days.

At the end of his personal spiritual renaissance, which lasted from nine to twelve days, Gheil began to experience his life and the world in a completely different way. He could see miracles everywhere. He saw and thought of everything he focused upon as good. He seemed to pull good toward himself like a magnet, he remembers.

Gheil sincerely believes it was at this point that his body started to respond. He refers to this time as his "spiritual tune-up." After this, he felt confident that he would simply be led to the things that he needed to do to become well in whatever way Christ wanted this wellness to emerge. Gheil was ready for anything; he had turned his life over to God completely. Gheil believes that the secret of self-healing is to find your purpose, and wellness will find you.

Today, over two years after the initial diagnosis, Gheil's doctors say there is no trace whatsoever of cancer in his body. Gheil sees this as a miracle and attributes his healing to the direct intervention of the Spirit in his life. He says he was ready for whatever wellness Christ decided for him, even if that was to be death. He knew full well that when he turned himself over to God, the outcome was out of his hands.

Day Eleven: Faith

Faith is unwavering and unconditional belief in and loyalty to God. Even though there is no earthly scientific proof that God exists, our spiritual experience demands, through our faith, that we have complete confidence in God's sustaining power.

A faithful person knows without doubt or question that God is there, indeed God is everywhere, in everything, and certainly within us. People of faith have strong convictions; they're steadfast and firm in their allegiance to God's wishes. They take seriously their duty to God and God's people. They are staunch and firm in their adherence to their genuine nature. Their word is binding; it's a promise. They give strong assurance. They are resolute and obedient; they have fidelity. Faithful persons live by a creed and expect that God is with them always. To be disloyal or false is the opposite of faith.

❧

Gheil's faith is personal and profound. He says, "My God is my life. He has promised me eternity, and that's exactly what I have right now!" Gheil's faith is specific. He encourages others, "Picture your cancer (or other sickness). Imagine your hand being led by God actually going into your body and plucking out that cancer spot or tumor. Have confidence that God's healing power is always at work and that you can assist in your wellness journey, whatever it may be."

Gheil proclaims that his faith is paramount to him. He says, "I'm really dumb about the mechanics of my religion, but I can ask God for anything and I have a true, God-given belief that he is always with me. The Father is the true Father of healing." For Gheil, there is only one place from which all healing comes. "God is full of miracles, and if we don't see them, it's our own fault," Gheil says.

Gheil relates in celebration: "No matter what happens, it happens for a purpose. My cancer has a purpose: to turn my life around. My cancer has shown me what living and loving is all about. You must have faith that God will heal you. Just like when you go to the store to buy a gallon of milk, you don't doubt that the milk will be there. You don't give it a second thought. You know that it will be there. By the same token, you simply know that God will heal you."

The question, of course, is what form this healing will take. "Your Spirit will guide you wherever you need to go," Gheil says. Gheil credits his growth in faith to his cancer. "God did not give me life to take it away. I will live forever. God wastes nothing. He certainly didn't create an entire universe just so a few men could gaze at it through their telescopes every six months!"

Meditations on Faith

MORNING

I place my faith in thoughts of light.

Today my thoughts are transformed. I place my faith in thoughts of light rather than dark. In the past, I have allowed my faith to go in opposite directions, and it hasn't worked for my spiritual development. Today I place my faith where it rightfully belongs. I bring my faith wherever I go because of the living Presence who walks with me in every situation. Faith unites me and rebuilds the fragments of doubt that had begun to overwhelm me.

AFTERNOON

Christ will place my faith where it belongs.

I offer my faith to Christ, confident that he will place it where it belongs. I ask you, holy Friend, to let me recover my full faith wherever I lost it. I have misplaced my faith in the past; today I find it again and use it for the most good. Help me, Lord, to have faith in that power that heals all pain. There are no bounds to the magnitude of the faith that heals.

EVENING

I am rocked to sleep in your cradle of faith.

Faith makes me whole. No limitations, no barriers, and no encumbrances can possibly stop faith from triumphing. Faith is dedicated to truth, and faith that has been misplaced in doubt will end only in pain. I am quiet now in my faith in the God who loves me. My faithful thinking moves my world closer to its source in you. Tonight my thoughts awaken as I am rocked to sleep in your cradle of faith.

Day Twelve: Wisdom

Wisdom can be defined several ways. The worldly definition of wisdom is "accumulated knowledge." However, knowledge alone does not provide wisdom. Getting closer to the Christian view, wisdom is the ability to discern inner qualities and relationships. The process of discernment is similar to the way in which the evangelist John teaches us to love by seeing the light of Christ in everyone.

Wisdom implies insight, good sense, or judgment. When one is guided by wise attitudes or follows a wise course of action, one is prudent, sane, and sensible. However, when one practices spiritual wisdom, one is profound, deep, and appreciative.

Wisdom includes knowing more than facts; it means being enlightened, illuminated, solid, and having the capacity to comprehend complicated situations and simplify them into a singular purpose, God's purpose. To be wise, one does not have to be erudite or scholarly. Rather, spiritual wisdom encompasses intuitiveness in the sense that one can "see into" a person, relationship, behavior, or situation and recognize God's presence there.

ॐ

Gheil sees wisdom in two forms. The first, what he terms "education," is tools for living learned from books. The second type of wisdom, for Gheil, is spiritual wisdom, which is not a skill or a fact but a spiritual enlightenment.

Gheil says wisdom is "an eternal thing…God's plan for how we climb his ladder." Our spirit self gains wisdom through experience. Wisdom is essential for healing. "We cannot be taught to be wise; we learn wisdom through spiritual development," says Gheil. "Wisdom means understanding the difference between the real and the unreal; spirit is real, everything else is unreal. Wisdom allows you to do the healing work you need to do, to ask God to help you. We can't heal ourselves alone," Gheil maintains. "We must build up our spiritual strength through prayer."

In his wisdom, Gheil recognizes that "symptoms, whatever they are, are ways of informing us where we need forgiveness. I know that I have a choice, to heal or not; I choose to heal, which means to accept what God's plan is for me. How is it that no one ever cries when we struggle, struggle, struggle, to come into this world, but we do cry when we struggle, struggle, struggle, to die? Is one any greater than the other? Being judgmental saps our healing spirit self. We need to accept God's plan and let go of the world."

Meditations on Wisdom

MORNING

Wisdom orders my thoughts.

As my body reminds me of its needs, I realize that only wisdom gives me the basis for ordering my thoughts. And my thoughts give me the internal communication necessary for healing. Disordered thoughts cannot assist my healing. Wisdom gives order and purpose to my life. My thoughts take me along wherever they go, to healing or to chaos. My thoughts produce something; I have no idle thoughts. Either my thoughts are wise and therefore of God or they are separate and therefore of this world.

AFTERNOON

My inner wisdom is teaching me.

Let me accept the wisdom of the best thoughts I have entertained. My inner wisdom is teaching me that I can learn lessons even from my sickness. I can therefore teach myself. I can share ideas and understand that in this sharing comes a strengthening that in itself is healing. My wisdom is my teacher today. I will listen and give back gratitude, which produces joy.

EVENING

I turn to my wise Source.

I hear wisdom in my silence. I listen and hear the depth and breath of the universe inside me. I listen to God's wisdom whispering to me of harmony, of health, and of healing. I turn to my wise Source. I marvel at his magnitude and find him awesome. Tonight I dream only of wise choices as I identify examples of wisdom in my life.

Day Thirteen: Love

The world teaches us that love is a feeling, a physical/emotional reaction of strong affection based on mutual admiration. The problem with such a definition is that it bases Christ's most important commandment on the transitory and shifting foundation of human emotion, which is shaky at best. The human view of love is something like "you scratch my back and I'll scratch yours." Such an impression is shortsighted at best and ultimately destructive. Love means much more than benevolence toward one's fellow humans and more than having common interests with another person. Christian love is demonstrated in the way we live the life of Jesus. It's an assurance, an enthusiastic devotion and unselfish loyalty, to seeing Christ in everyone. Loving means adoring God, thriving on his promises to us, and cherishing his people as other children of God.

To be loving is to be naive and may mean being disliked or even scorned. It means holding most dear the principles of holiness, blessedness, and wholeness that is Christ. To love means to value God and God's ways above all else. Love is our unwavering decision that Christ is the absolute center of our lives. In short, to love means to adore Jesus. The opposite of human love is hatred, while the opposite of Christian love is fear.

Gheil speaks of little else but love. It seems hard for him to put together a sentence without "love" in it somewhere. It is almost as if no matter what he is talking about, his real message is love. Gheil demonstrates love in many ways. "One thing my cancer taught me," says Gheil, "is to continuously give God praise and thanksgiving. I thank God every day for the strength to get out of bed."

In addition to this obvious praise, Gheil shows love in other unique ways. For example, he has insight into what he calls "spiritual senses." Just as the body has five senses that enable us to gather data about the world, our spirit selves have spiritual senses. Gheil claims that when we are spiritually attuned, we can actually smell "a wonderful spiritual aroma coming not only from ourselves but from others as well."

Spiritually, he maintains, we can see more with our eyes closed than we can with them open. Spiritual vision is separate from physical sight. Gheil relates that Jesus always touched when he healed. "This is a lesson for us, that we are to touch one another and touch ourselves." Likewise, we can taste the Spirit and hear the sound of the universe when we encounter love in our lives.

Another interesting facet of love that Gheil outlines concerns our path toward self-healing. In order to heal, we must love ourselves, and in order to love ourselves, we must cleanse ourselves of any injustices. Gheil asks, "Is there anything left undone in your life? Are you holding any grievances? Are you experiencing any inner conflict? Are you forgetting your spiritual nature? What really needs healing within you? What is truly broken? Which of these requires your attention? Make sure you attend to them or healing will be blocked." Your lifestyle or your inner conflicts may have tilled the inner soil of your self in such a way that illness could take root there. "Love enables you to get your life back under spiritual control," says Gheil.

Meditations on Love

MORNING

Today I think only thoughts of love.

My prayer today is of love, which always answers. I call on love, which is unable to deny my call for help. Love hears my pain and rises to find a solution to it. Today I vault over the barriers I have erected against love: my grievances, my judgments, my blaming. Today I think only thoughts of love.

AFTERNOON

I now recognize what is real to love.

I am created in the likeness of love. My true reality is only of love. Love reaches every part of me. It illuminates every corner of my dark soul, and it transforms my thoughts of failure to thoughts of success. I am drawn to love. All my behaviors are motivated by love, but now I recognize what is real for me to love.

EVENING

I resolve to exempt no one from my love.

As shadows grow long, I resolve to exempt no one from my love. That would be like making the Holy Spirit unwelcome in part of my mind. I extend love throughout my being. Love nestles into every cell that may be sick, injecting a healing balm of heaven into it, giving it celestial relief. How wonderful is my healing, how marvelous its results.

Day Fourteen: Wholeness

To be whole is to have integrity in the sense of being intact, complete, and undivided. Wholeness means the sum total, the entire unit, unbroken and lacking no part. Wholeness is the unmodified and undiminished entirety of something. A person who is whole is complete and total, concentrated on one goal, and directed toward one end. To the spiritually whole person, that one end is love as embodied in Christ Jesus. To be whole is to express our full nature and total development in God. We are healed in God when we are whole in the sense that no part of us is unconnected to the source of healing; no member or part of the entirety is working without being in concert with every other part or member.

In Christian wholeness, we operate from the faith position of consecration, knowing that every child of God is like ourselves and, therefore, cannot be in even the remotest way separated from us. Unity in Christ is the mark of Christian wholeness. Recognizing that the children of God form a collective unity of indivisible love, an aggregate of integrated and seamless togetherness, is the ultimate goal of wholeness. We are not detached from God in any way.

Even though we exist on this material plane, no separation exists, no alienation is possible, no division from our true reality in the Spirit is conceivable. We are all working together as one, even though the opposite appears true. The opposite of wholeness is fragmentation, chaos, and partition.

❧

Gheil relates, "I found my Christ after I was told I was going to die." This jolt of reality prompted Gheil to become present and focused. "I wanted Christ right now, today. I wanted to feel good with my Christ today." To be whole, we must guide our minds away from the external reality of the world and direct it toward love, which has the only power to heal. Gheil suggests that you picture your sickness inside you as a force that divides rather than allows you to remain whole. "Picture yourself going into your body, grabbing your sickness, removing it, and throwing it away," says Gheil. "This is something you can do with God's help." Wholeness means you never have to feel lonely, because you have found the love of the Spirit within you.

Another aspect of wholeness, reminds Gheil, is the wonderful healing power of laughter. "Laugh every day; laugh in praise of his name. This will help remove the sickness from you." In order to achieve wholeness, "we must learn to separate what's happening to us physically from what's happening spiritually," says Gheil. Even though this separation appears contradictory to the idea of wholeness, it's the beginning of recognizing your true reality — the only reality that has the power to heal you. In Gheil's mind, when sick people contemplate suicide, it is a product or symptom of lack of wholeness.

Sickness is "a slap in the face," says Gheil. It shakes your sense of integrity and your definition of who you are as nothing else can. Gheil becomes fervent when he speaks of wholeness and thankfulness. "I'm so thankful to be well each morning when I wake up. I've found my purpose. I walk in the Spirit all through the day." Wholeness demands that you cast away any "hang-ups" left over from your childhood. Move to get rid of any grievances by confessing them and seeking forgiveness. "Otherwise," says Gheil, "we will continue to do things 'not of the Spirit.' "

Meditations on Wholeness

MORNING

I learn of healing through wholeness.

This morning I remember God. I appreciate his wholeness and take great solace that his wholeness extends to me. There is no separation between us. I learn of healing through wholeness. Wholeness heals me because it connects my mind with the mind of God; indeed, they are one. Today my thoughts are of wholeness because I see it everywhere. Wholeness is invisible, but I can learn it.

AFTERNOON

I am whole, just as I am right now.

The Holy Spirit teaches wholeness. When wholeness is fully recognized, no more healing is necessary. Today I seek to understand the wholeness of the Father. When I do, I will be healed. In every part of me is the wholeness of God. Wholeness is a gift I have already been given. I am whole, just as I am right now.

EVENING

Tonight I sleep in whole peace.

God remembers me as I drift into sleep tonight. What God remembers must be whole. I am made whole simply because I desire it. My sickness is brought to its knees when I perceive my wholeness with God. I accept who I am, and in that instant I am made whole. My wholeness expands as I grow in spiritual power. Wholeness heals my wounds and eases my pain so I can sleep in peace. Tonight I sleep in whole peace.

Day Fifteen: Charity

Charity means benevolent goodwill given unconditionally, without expecting anything in return. Charity in its fullest sense is implicitly helpful. Charity is the ability to recognize the needs of another and work selflessly to meet those needs. Charity is generous and liberally given. It is forgiving and altruistic. Charity is big-hearted giving in the most authentic of Christian traditions. The opposite of charity is malice, ill will, malevolence, and taking away.

ε.

Once again we see an individualistic expression of virtue with Gheil. Charity means giving to others, and for Gheil this means giving them a piece of his heart. "Picture your heart many, many, many times bigger than your body. Whenever anyone comes into your life, make sure you give that person some of your heart — your love."

Gheil seeks ways of offering love to everyone. "See how many people you can give love to in one day; give them each a piece of your heart. Love goes in them and is reflected and extended to everyone. Soon you have trainloads of love going everywhere," Gheil relates with excitement. "Giving away your love in perfect charity is the easiest way of finding your spirit. Extend your healing to others who may also be sick; bless them with your spirit."

Gheil lives the spirit of charity. "Be kind and gentle to people," he recommends. "Listen to what they are saying, even between the lines." In giving, you are actually receiving, and here is the fountainhead of healing. Gheil admonishes us to "relax with Jesus Christ every hour. He will not desert you in your time of need. Walk with him always. He is the light of the world."

Charity enables Gheil to surmount any personal trauma he may be experiencing. "When you help another, your own woes go away. If you have a migraine headache and help someone who has cut a finger, your headache goes away." Eventually, he says, "you get to a point where you are simply exploding with love, and anyone in your path can't help but get a piece of your heart."

Meditations on Charity

MORNING

I am struck by the abundance of God.

As I awaken, I am struck by the abundance God has given me. I reminisce about the many, many gifts I have been given. Today I appreciate these gifts and my sense of abundance continues to this very instant. This is what it means to be charitable. When I recognize the charity that has pervaded my life, and continues to do so, then can I exercise charity.

AFTERNOON

I am charitable to myself.

Charity is a way of thinking that allows me to see others as deserving of my gifts. I see that I am likewise deserving of my gifts, which are actually God's gifts to me. Today I will acknowledge that I need help and commit to accepting the help I need. I am charitable to myself.

EVENING

Charity sees the perfection in me.

Charity, like all virtues, reflects love. Charity is of God, but in this world. Love is of God and is God. Healing rests on charity, because sickness is of this world. Charity allows me to see not only my human need but also my spiritual perfection. I am not limited; my sickness is.

Thought Prayer

Let me remember constantly that your healing power is in my mind. This power is the central healing force in the universe. I have absolute faith in this power and have every right to seize upon it as my inheritance. The surety of the great love that I know dwells within me renders all my former doubts meaningless. Let me always use the wisdom that is my endowment in ways that enlighten my mind; help me discern the profound silence I possess through you. I delight in the deep understanding that I have found my only true goal in you. The road before me is paved with fruits of love, wholeness, and charity, fallen from trees of faith and wisdom. As I look to heaven, I recognize peace at last and feel its soft embrace surround my heart and mind with forgiveness and with love.

Today I set aside for you, my inner Teacher, times of quiet that I may hear your instructions of healing in peace, beyond the world's rattle, and recognize whatever meaning you wish to infuse into my thoughts. My mind rests in the Holy Spirit, who offers me this single freedom: I am free today. The dark night that formerly enshrouded my thoughts is over now. I have come to your light. I trust in your faith, your wisdom, your love, your wholeness, and your charity and strive to incorporate these virtue-gifts into my soul. Daily I come to the sacred place inside to spend holy time with you, my faithful loving Friend, and to share my dream of unity with you, long forgotten but now remembered. Amen.

Chapter Five

FEELINGS

How we feel is not the consequence of what is happening in our lives, but rather the result of how we interpret what is happening in our lives.

Introduction

In the midst of serious illness, it is normal to feel hate, fear, and anger: hate that things have to be this way, fear that they will only get worse, and anger that no one seems capable of helping. Somehow, however, we know in our hearts that the darkness gripping our emotions is but a deception. It is as if we somehow need the hate, fear, and anger merely to cover up the lonely feeling that we're all by ourselves.

This loneliness violates an internal sense that someone should be there to help us. But such deception only makes us feel even more fearful — fearful that the deception may be found out. So we work hard and exert tremendous energy to establish the reality of the hate, fear, and anger and to justify hanging on to them. And the struggle continues.

How we feel is not the consequence of what is happening in our lives but the result of how we interpret what is happening in our lives. Anthony Robbins, the human development specialist quoted in Chapter Two, says there are two kinds of states we can find ourselves in. The first he calls *enabling states*. Enabling states are characterized by confidence, love, inner strength, joy, ecstasy, and other positive feelings. These states are enabling, Robbins says, because these feelings tap into great wellsprings of personal power for us.

Robbins calls the second kind of states *paralyzing states*. He describes these as ones which produce such negative feelings as confusion, depression, fear, anxiety, sadness, and frustration. These emotions, says Robbins, leave us feeling powerless.

Many times we can feel lost in the deepest part of ourselves. In our heart of hearts, we feel like orphans here in this world, abandoned for no apparent reason and destined to feel pain and suffering. From time to time, however, we feel a soft pang within that pulls us like a magnet to our true spiritual home. We can make a hundred homes here on this earth and yet not settle our feelings of restlessness for someplace else.

There is a child within who seeks the divine Parent's house and feels like an alien here on earth. Yet it is in the very defenselessness of this child that our true strength really lies. This child lights the world. This child is eternal, without limits, speaking to us unendingly of home and beckoning us to go, too. Find rest with this child, nurture and nourish the child with peaceful respite.

When we feel lost, our child is lost in the world, where a mist of shifting dreams and fearful thoughts blind us and cause us to feel unsteady, vulnerable, insecure, unconscious, and afraid. A time of sickness is such a time of feeling lost. In sickness there is both fear and respite. To be sure, sickness is unsettling; vulnerability is its primary emotional fruit. Yet we still are called to look beyond this paralyzing state and find the richness resting there and waiting patiently for us to nurture it to glorious life in Christ.

Emotional Pain: What You Can Do Each time you feel the stab of pain caused by these paralyzing emotions, realize that you are holding the knife and that you yourself are plunging it. This knife is your thoughts of condemnation as you remain asleep to the reality of Christ and his new and rejuvenating message of love. Your sickness can act as the catalyst for awakening into spiritual consciousness.

Emotional pain is your signal that some unforgiveness is lying deep in your mind. Release the pain by reframing the thought that produced it in the first place. God does not will that you suffer; God wills that you find the truth. God helps you forgive the thousand-and-one faults with which you blame and discredit yourself. Humility does not mean condemnation or denial; it simply means the truth.

How can you see your illness as your friend? When you regard it as your enemy and fight against it, you only ensure that it remains with you; fighting a war always depletes you. When you recognize your illness but call it your friend, you not only accept it but also gain energy from it to do the real work on this earth you are called to do. When you attack, you will be sad. Entrust your illness to God. Become defenseless and feel the strength come back to you.

Deep inside you is your holiness: that silent, sacred place where pain is no longer, where all sorrow ends, and where all problems are solved. You are holy because your reality is of God. Your holiness makes you whole; it makes no demands of you. Your physical self sees you as separate and therefore incomplete. Consequently, it sees only demands and lacks. Demands produce a feeling of deficit, restlessness, and indecision. You feel strong when you can see past the way things appear to be, when you can keep a steady gaze upon the light that lies behind outer appearances.

Dr. Siegel proposes that one reason people convert themselves into patients and feel great physical and emotional pain is that they try to make their world — or at least the persons around them — happy. Over time, they forfeit their own happiness by denying their own feelings and concentrating on the feelings of their loved ones with a misplaced sympathy. We need, instead, he says, to develop the courage to be ourselves, honestly and genuinely, and to express our feelings forthrightly. Otherwise, we will add to the burden of illness in our lives.

Norman Cousins reviewed literally thousands of medical research reports from all over the globe and came to a similar decision about repressed feelings. He maintained that repressed feelings, especially when they were sufficiently repressed to produce clinical depression, clearly had a negative impact on the body's normal and natural resistance to disease. Cousins wrote, "This conclusion was strengthened by their [researchers'] observation that relief from depression is paralleled by changes in the immune system."

Grace's Story

The following is an abridged account of the story Grace, age fifty, related.

"One morning, two years ago, I awoke aghast to find a lump the size of an egg protruding from a spot just to the right of my breastbone. I had noticed for some time that a small ridgelike bump had made its presence known, too, but I thought it was a simple cyst. Having suffered with fibrocystic disease for some time, I thought this was just more of it. Perhaps this was my denial at work. When my doctor saw the egg-sized lump, he was crestfallen. Immediately, he questioned me about how long it had been there. I was embarrassed to tell him I had noticed it a full year earlier, only to dismiss it as 'nothing.'

"The next day he had me on the operating table. He had warned me that he would probably have to perform a mastectomy, but that, thank God, wasn't necessary. Six weeks later I was back on the table, and this time he took the nodes that were cancerous. I went home from that surgery on Christmas Eve. It was then I found a new life.

"Now I can look back and realize that my breast cancer was a beautiful and comforting gift. Certainly, I didn't think so when I was receiving my chemotherapy and radiation treatments, nor when I lost my hair, suffered extreme fatigue, and became totally dependent for the first time in my life. During these times, I was full of fear, desperation, and sorrow. But now I can see that God lives in each of us and wants us to love and help one another.

"Before my cancer, I was a faithful person, but my faith had become routine. Certainly, it was routine as compared to the faith I enjoy now in my life. Initially, I felt a certain 'loneliness' because I was dealing with the disease alone, in the sense that I alone was the victim. These feelings, however, quickly vanished as God's grace began to reveal itself to me more and more."

Day Sixteen: Joyfulness

To be joyful is to gain great pleasure or delight and to express it in celebration. To be joyful is to show great happiness, a glad heart, and exuberant gaiety. Spiritual joy is the unspoken inner knowledge that God is your true reality, even though you dwell on this plane where pain, loss, meanness, suffering, and deprivation seem to be all around. To be joyful is to be expressively jubilant or inwardly elated.

Christian joyfulness is triumphant and delightful; it is a jubilee, a highly spirited happening; it is an inner quiet and an insightful meditation; it is a special prayer of thanksgiving. Joyfulness is the emotional response to the knowledge that God's grace is sustaining you in perfection and that it is all you will ever need. Furthermore, joyfulness is the result of knowing that you will have the full measure of God's grace throughout your life on this plane.

૨৯

Grace expresses it this way: "My joy has come from knowing my God is with me, knowing I'm not alone. Once I turned so completely and humbly to God for help, a sense of serenity prevailed through a healing period of mind and body.

"When our friendships are such that we take time to listen and understand what our loved ones are experiencing, we are giving a priceless gift of ourselves. Just as I've had friends laugh at a circumstance in my life, I have also had them break down and cry in an overwhelming feeling of empathy and compassion. It has created such a bond with these persons that even when they're not with me, I feel the companionship of their souls. How sad it is that people get so busy, so caught up in their own lives, that their friendships become casual Christmas cards and brief phone calls. Sometimes it takes a tragedy to make us see the goodness of God."

Meditations on Joyfulness

MORNING

I celebrate your presence in me, Lord.

Lord, as I begin this day of learning to love you better, I feel your delightful care wash over me. I am thankful that I live in your luxuriant garden of grace. I celebrate your presence within me and feel my heart jump with gaiety as I greet you today with a glad heart filled with expression.

AFTERNOON

Your delight resides in me.

I am jubilant as I think of your marvelous care for me. I see your healing power caress my broken parts, and I am elated with joy knowing you are working within me. All turmoil, chaos, and tension is draining from me and being replaced with your triumphant delight. Your light of joy operates miracles in my life and I'm joyous.

EVENING

I am filled with the light of your joy.

As the night embraces the land, your joy surrounds my soul. I rest in your inner guidance and find respite in your peace. I offer my special prayer of thanksgiving, knowing your sustaining power will continue its marvelous work within me all through the night. I am filled with the light of your joy.

Day Seventeen: Trust

To be trusting is to be confident. It is the assured reliance upon God's healing power to bring us through adversity. To be trusting is to have a mature dependence upon the kindness and compassion that God's love will ever be manifested in our lives. Trust engenders hope that Christ's promise is now being fulfilled, regardless of how our human eyes may perceive man's inhumanity to man. Trust allows us to know that we have a right to be here no less than all God's other creations.

Trust teaches responsibility and presupposes relationship. It allows us to place ourselves in the charge of God and to let go of the worldly control we feel we must hold on to. Trust means to rely on, to believe in, and to expect with confidence. It assumes credibility and bespeaks anticipation of good things to come. To trust is to consign our lives to God's care and to recognize that God works through his children.

"To trust in God," says Grace, "you must give up your life and its direction and surrender to his will. In any serious accident or illness, I believe we can be reduced to a childlike dependence upon those around us — friends, family, nurses, doctors. God will see you through your suffering and pain. It is true; he knows how much we can bear, and he won't ask more of us.

"Each of us is unique and possesses special qualities. If we look from this perspective, we can see that just as each flower has its scent, its own shape, its own color, each individual has a strength, a quality, a virtue, that is expressed in a way unlike the way it is seen in anyone else. Through my illness and recent hardships, my friends were my gifts from God. I have learned and gained from each of them. The spiritual tonic they supplied is a nurturance sent by God as the nectar for my healing. Just as our bodies can restore themselves, we are here to help restore and rebuild the spiritual growth in one another. When serious illness and other problems present themselves, we sometimes feel lost and alone in our weakness. God is everywhere; all we must do is look.

"I can honestly say that since I had cancer, I'm not afraid to die. Before…I was afraid. As a result of my cancer, I realized for the first time in my life how God truly helps us through other people. He often speaks to us this way. He encourages, comforts, and reasons with us. Until we all see this as our purpose here, we are lost. How can we compare the problems or pain we have to what God feels for us as his children? I believe our lives have a plan; I can look back on my situation and see how God has protected me. Our problems are not caused by God but by ourselves."

Meditations on Trust

MORNING

My trust is nowhere but with you today.

My eyes open and my soul stirs to awaken my mind today. Help me trust my brothers and sisters today, for as I trust the good in them, I give my trust to the good in me. Today let me not only have the good intent to feel the illusion of trust, let me convert my intentions into action so I can feel your trust working in me in a permanent, genuine way. My trust is nowhere but with you today.

AFTERNOON

I can learn to trust profoundly.

I look upon all those who come to me as messengers of Christ. I trust in their message. I know my heart leaps with trust as I recognize your healing words on their tongues, your healing vision in their eyes, your healing touch in their hands, and your healing sweetness on their lips. I cannot trust a little; I can only trust fully and robustly. I trust in others as your children and my instructors. My, how I can learn to trust so profoundly!

EVENING

All my problems are resolved...I trust.

All my problems are resolved...I trust. Swirling within my heart, I feel the thrill of trust as it settles all my cares and drowns all my fears. I am authentically willing now, as I never have been before, that whatever else enters into me this night will be solved. The Holy Spirit is profoundly with me, thoroughly capturing my reality in her trusting embrace. I am safe through this night.

Day Eighteen: Being a Love-finder

To be a love-finder is to recognize God's hand in everyone and in everything. Love-finders awaken in the morning and immediately seek ways of seeing God throughout the day. A love-finder finds love and its derivatives; a fault-finder finds criticism, blame, judgment, or guilt. Which would you rather be?

A love-finder discovers God's presence. Love-finding may be hard work, not because love isn't all around, but because we are so well-trained by the world to be fault-finders. It seems so much easier for us to find negativism than to find the reality of God. Therefore, being a love-finder requires searching and effort, study and experiment, thorough toil and elegant life management. We find love in our experience; we need to detect it in ourselves and those around us.

❧

Not long after Grace's first operation, she decided to stay after Mass to pray one dark, rainy morning. She lit a candle before the Blessed Virgin, asking her for help. Then she rose to leave. The church was empty as Grace walked slowly down the center aisle, head down, steadying herself on the pews as she made way to the rear of the church. By the time she reached the vestibule, she was crying as she put on her coat and scarf.

Thinking she was alone, she put her tear-streaked face in her hands and simply sobbed. Suddenly, she heard footsteps. Raising her eyes, she looked into the face of an older woman. The woman's face seemed to Grace to be the most radiant, the sweetest, kindest face she had ever seen. Then the stranger wrapped her arms around Grace in an embrace of reassurance and said, "Honey, everything is going to be all right."

As quickly as she had appeared, the woman left. Grace was too flabbergasted to speak. She remembers thinking that the woman's hug felt as if the Blessed Mother was hugging her. After a search of the surrounding streets, Grace found the woman walking down the sidewalk. "I'll never forget what you did for me," Grace said. The woman replied — and now Grace could see scars on her face that she later learned were caused by cancer surgery — "We all have to reach out to one another."

Grace felt as though she had seen God on earth. Something within her shifted, and she knew she would be all right. "Here was an undeniable sign from God," she thought. She had been desperate and depressed as she walked down the aisle of the church; as she put it, "A human soul could not have felt more down." After her encounter with the radiant woman, Grace felt as though Christ had singled her out to receive his grace. "I'm so grateful," she relates. "I often think of her."

Grace advises: "When you awaken each morning, resolve to find love throughout the day. Love is everywhere, it's the primary motive force in the universe, and it's our job as Christians to see it in action everywhere."

Love surrounds us and is inside us...feel it...see it. When you're puzzled about your behavior or that of others, ask yourself, "What makes that person do what he or she is doing?" You will soon understand, if you can trace the details of the action back to the most basic motivators, that all behavior is based on either love or fear. The fear we feel is simply fear that we will lose love. So, in effect, love (or the fear of its loss) motivates everything we do. Dr. Gerald Jampolsky says it best: "All that we do is either a statement of love or a request for love." There is no doubt that we are called to be love-finders in a most practical yet profound sense. Your healing, your very wellness, is dependent on your ability to recognize the love that is all around you.

Meditations on Being a Love-finder

MORNING

Love is everywhere today.

As I open my eyes today, divine Guide, let me also open my heart. Let me feel the love you have planted there when I was yet a thought of your love. Let me touch this seedling of love in my heart and feel it extend its comforting branches over my world all day. Love is everywhere today.

AFTERNOON

I am no longer a fault-finder.

How immature I have been to seek what's wrong rather than see love. Today I will see "what's right." God's rightness surrounds me. My brokenness is but a means of letting your love pour from me and through me. I feel its refreshing, cleansing, healing balm bathe me in perfection.

EVENING

Love pulsates through me.

I can close my eyes and see your love as it pulsates through your creations, Lord. I am part of your creation, in tune with your creation. Your love drives the universe and drives me as part of it. I praise your purpose; I feel your marvelous meaning. I know all is well. I no longer doubt your reasons for current changes in my life.

Day Nineteen: Empathy

To be empathetic (or empathic) is to have the capacity to participate in the feelings or ideas of another person. The noted counselor Dr. Carl Rogers referred to this quality as "walking in another's moccasins." In the movie *Gandhi*, a Muslim asked the great Indian leader how the strife between Muslims and Hindus would ever cease. Gandhi responded to this sincere but pained man that he could adopt an orphaned Hindu child and raise him or her to be a good Hindu while residing in his own Muslim home.

Empathy is the ability to recognize fully what another person is communicating and to see the experiences and feelings being communicated as the other person sees and feels them. Empathy means going beyond the facts of the communication, focusing clearly on them, and "being with" them emotionally. Empathy includes striving continuously for a deeper and more thorough understanding of the other person's perspective. Gandhi's advice to the Muslim man was an intimate lesson in empathy: to raise a child to adulthood in an alien faith. Here, thought Gandhi, was the formula for healing a nation. So, too, empathy can be part of your formula for self-healing.

Empathy is sometimes incorrectly confused with sympathy. Sympathy is the ability to offer a compassionate response to the unfortunate experience of another. Sympathy involves reacting to the misfortune of another. Empathy, by contrast, involves "tuning in" to the deepest feelings being experienced by another. Empathy includes becoming acutely aware of the totality of feelings being communicated either verbally or nonverbally. Sympathy is a simple emotional, often sentimental, response such as "I'm sorry for your trouble." Empathy is a profound expression of emotional intimacy which says, "I can feel your feelings."

Grace shows her empathy primarily in two ways. The first is her ability to understand fully what another person is saying to her. Grace can go far beyond the actual meaning of the words being expressed. She seems clearly aware of the other person's belief core, value system, and attitudes; she can perceive the world as the other person does; she can assume the same thinking and feeling patterns. Finally, she knows intuitively the decisions and actions the other will take. Grace is not clairvoyant; she simply has fine-tuned her natural virtue of empathy, primarily as a result of her cancer. She is uncannily aware of the sum total of the message other people are conveying. As she knows others at deeper levels, she comes to understand her own spiritual nature in a similar way.

The second aspect of empathy Grace has grown proficient in is what is known as reflection of feelings. Not only can she discern the content being expressed, she can go even further by identifying the implicit feelings beneath the words. Feelings are the emotional underpinnings of living; they drive the drama of life. Empathy is used effectively when the listener can identify and feed back to the speaker feelings heard with the "third ear."

Grace's ability to reflect feelings is obvious in her reports of the special qualities she sees in each of her friends. Such discernment requires someone who not only can cooperate and participate but who is also unafraid to compliment others for their special qualities or behaviors.

Meditations on Empathy

MORNING

Empathy gives me rest and time to heal.

The sun brightens my room, and I greet another day of healing. I am drawn by empathy to understand the feeling depths of my brothers and sisters, not to be drawn into their suffering, whatever it may be, but to demonstrate God's healing in my own experience. My empathy for them directs my attention away from my own struggles and gives me rest and time to heal.

AFTERNOON

My empathy strengthens me.

As I lift my feelings beyond myself and let them rest awhile, I think of those whose lives have been stung by tragedy. Yet my thoughts do not weaken me; in fact, they do the opposite. My empathy strengthens me, because I sit quietly by and let the Holy Spirit relate strength to others through me. I am but a channel, a spark of light in Christ's discipleship.

EVENING

Empathy lets me see today.

Today is almost over and my healing has progressed well. Yet I live in the now, not in the past. My empathy is now; I don't relive old heartaches or recall old tragedies. I remember with honesty and reality. Sometimes the outer manifestations of my emotions failed to communicate what I intended; yet I wanted the best for everyone, always. Empathy lets me see today and frame yesterday as it really was.

Day Twenty: Gratitude

Gratitude means expressing a profound thankfulness for all God has given us. Gratitude recognizes and appreciates the giftedness of our lives and instills a sense of indebtedness to God for those gifts. Gratitude offers praise, acknowledges grace and honor, and renders us worshipful for the unmerited divine assistance we have inherited as children of God. Gratitude includes a continuous praise, a marvelous prayer of thanksgiving, and a pious benediction that offers worship and adoration with a sense of sanctified obligation to do God's will.

The prayer of gratitude is simple; it is the great "Thank you, Lord!" Spiritual gratitude recognizes that everything that exists is actually our teacher in that it illuminates our way to God. Can you recognize your illness as a teacher and offer God thanks and praise as a result? The gratitude is not for the sickness itself but for what the Holy Spirit holds out in loving healing as a result of it.

&

"My friends are gifts from God; they're my spiritual tonic," says Grace. "My cancer allowed me to see the many gracious gifts in other people in an entirely new light. The greatest gift God has given me is to see him in people all around me. My emotional pain was much greater, much more intense, than any physical pain I felt with my cancer. There's no pill or shot you can take for the emotional pain…friends and family are my best medicine.

"My cancer actually made a better person out of me. I learned so much," Grace relates in absolute gratitude. "And so much of it has helped me live a richer, fuller life beyond my cancer. Everyone has special gifts. Some have the gift of patience, others the gift of understanding. I never saw my own gifts so clearly as I have since my cancer.

"For example, I have learned to pray in a very different way. Before my cancer, I'd simply recited the prayers I learned in grammar school: the Our Father, the Hail Mary, the Glory to the Father, the Acts of Faith, Hope, and Love. I could repeat them verbatim without hesitation. My spiritual development was still back in grade school. Now I pray from my heart in gratitude. My prayers are ones of thanks and praise. I feel so much better when I pray regularly and pray in gratitude," Grace concludes.

Meditations on Gratitude

MORNING

I appreciate this day of healing.

I awake in awesome appreciation for God's healing work within me. Unless I am grateful, I will fail to appreciate what is my inheritance. I am filled with gratitude for my brothers and sisters, for their loving thoughts and for their work to help me. Each of them brings me more deeply into my awareness, and this also gratifies me as I dedicate this day to healing.

AFTERNOON

My gratitude is unspeakable.

I am touched to know another person, because in but one moment of genuine recognition of another's holy self, I am allowed to touch my own holy self and feel the unity — the absolute lack of separation — that God has intended for us. My gratitude is unspeakable; there are no words to express it. The feeling in me pours out; I cannot contain it, for it runs like a refreshing spring from my soul, healing all in its wake.

EVENING

God's great rays of light heal me.

My gratitude allows me to see great rays of God's light extend back into darkness and forward into my soul. Like lasers, they pierce my fragile flesh and penetrate my brokenness, mending it and making me whole. I fall asleep with this image impressed on me. I feel the giant beams of light ferret out my disbelief and weld me together, clean and whole.

Feelings Prayer

Let me be still a moment and go home, for I feel alien here outside the persistent sweetness I remember, though sometimes as no more than a tiny throb deep inside. Divine Healer, help me to lay down my weapons of fear, anger, and hate. Allow me to find your joy, your trust, your love-finding, your empathy, and your gratitude. Give me rest, and let me listen to the child within who would take me home. Today I accept this child's defenselessness in exchange for all the toys of battle I have made. Help me, Lord, to be strong so I can see the truth and shine with the great rays of light inside me.

My strength sees only through Christ's eyes; it does not see the small, the weak, the sickly, and the dying that my human eyes see within myself. My strength does not see the helpless and afraid side of me, nor the poor, the sad, the starving, or the joyless parts of me. All these are but judgments I no longer need. My strength feels only the opposite of these in addition to abundance, plenty, and the joyful celebration of membership in the family of God. I am at home in you, Lord; I am not an alien but your natural holy child. I cherish my home and the healing balm of your love, warming my heart and penetrating to my soul. I rest untroubled, sure that only good can come to me. The stillness of my soul remains untouched and untroubled by the shrill, strident, frantic efforts of the world to wrestle me from my center in you. Amen.

Chapter Six

DECISIONS

We need to choose continuously to communicate to ourselves that our illness, indeed everything that has happened in our lives, and will happen, occurs for a purpose.

Introduction

Who is in charge of your free will, your world self or your holy self? Can you imagine what your free will looks like? If your free will were a person, what would it look like? Try to actually picture it in your mind's eye.

We need to choose continuously to communicate to ourselves that our illness, indeed everything that has happened in our lives, and will happen, occurs for a purpose.

Do you want to decide to be right or to be happy? If you wish to be happy, here are the rules for making decisions that lead to happiness.

1. Make no decisions by yourself. You are choosing not to be the judge of what to do.
2. Decide what kind of day you want and prepare for it to be given to you. Periodically, remind yourself throughout the day what kind of a day you would like.
3. When you feel uneasy, remember that you have unknowingly made a decision by yourself on your own terms. Try to give the decision to the Holy Spirit.
4. If you can't give the decision to the Holy Spirit, you can begin to change your mind with this statement: "At least I can decide that I do not like what I feel right now."
5. Now make this request: "I want another way to look at this."
6. Finally ask, "What can I lose by asking?"

You cannot suffer emotional pain unless it is your own decision; no emotional pain is possible unless your choice made it possible. You can feel nothing without the consent of your own choosing.

Actually, although the distinctions and possibilities of choice seem innumerable and endless, they boil down to one simple decision: *Do I choose love or do I choose fear? Do I choose life or do I choose death? Do I choose God or do I choose the world?* These are all the same decision. How does this apply to your sickness?

Decide today to take your rightful place as the collaborator with God running your life. Surrendering to him — choosing to allow him to lead the way — is your constant choice. The power of decision is your own. In a sense, this world is a great classroom where you are continuously challenged to make the right choice.

Whatever you decide for action, make sure that you choose in love. Your specific decision cannot be wrong if it is a decision for love. For example, suppose a middle-aged man confronts his wife with the statement, "You didn't put out my tennis shorts, and you put out the short summer socks instead of my longer winter socks!" How is his wife to respond if she wishes to do so in love?

She has a number of choices. Her first response choice might be "Yes, of course, I'll fix it right away, dear!" Second, she might respond, "You know, I feel rather discounted when you say things like that; you make it sound as though I don't care about you at all." Third, she may respond, "In love, I want to ask you to pick out your own tennis clothes in the future."

Regardless of the response you would have chosen in this situation — and regardless of what your position might be on male/female, husband/wife relations — none of these three responses is implicitly wrong. None of them is unloving; each has its own way of expressing love and each, therefore, can be viewed as an expression of love.

Become keenly aware of the many, many decisions you have to make, even about the thoughts and feelings you choose to give yourself. Each time you must make a decision, decide first to call upon the name of God in prayer. Listen to the voice within. Words are insignificant when you call upon the Father's name as a son or a daughter of God, for then the Father's thoughts become your own.

You have been given the power of decision, of free will, as a means of letting go of misperceptions and misthoughts. Deciding to forgive is the means by which the fear of death is overcome. Perhaps you need to forgive yourself for believing the misperception that at some psychic level you mistook your body to be your self. To whatever degree you believed in the world rather than in God, you invested in fear rather than in love.

You can make the decision to change an attitude by deciding to change your way of thinking on a certain subject. Think a new thought over and over again and you will transform it into an attitude. In so doing, you will transform your life.

Healing requires that you decide to look upon everything with love. Your expressions of love are your means to healing. Healing means letting go. When you give love, you receive love; and when you let go of fear, you free yourself to express love.

We make decisions from a series of options based upon our priorities, objectives, and goals. We also decide which strategies we will employ to achieve these goals. Decisions represent what we have decided we want. Decisions convert dreams and possibilities into potential action. Decisions are like headlights on our car; on a dark night, we can't safely drive anywhere without them.

Life is made up of decisions, decisions, and more decisions. You cannot act as codirector with God of your life without making decisions. Not making a decision is actually making one. You cannot stand still; you must change, and for this you need decisions. You need to make decisions constantly; without decisions you cannot grow; you cannot heal.

Only by dealing healthfully with your feelings can you make accurate decisions that produce healing. You have the option of making healthy or unhealthy decisions about your feelings.

Some unhealthy decisions about feelings are

- to "stuff" them
- to resist, fight, or deny them
- to project them onto someone or something else
- to disguise them, usually as some other feeling

Healthy decisions about feelings are

- to express them directly
- to consciously decide to do nothing
- to allow your feelings to wash over you
- to diffuse them by changing the thoughts that generated them in the first place

Stella's Story

Stella Hernandez describes herself as a country girl. "I grew up picking berries, washing beans, and stepping on rattlesnakes and copperheads. I never got bit though. See how God was with me even then, even when I didn't know it?"

Now at age fifty-seven, Stella looks back on what she describes as a "wonderful childhood." Her father died when she was in the first grade, and

"Mama remarried when I was in the fourth. We didn't know we were poor; you don't miss what you never had," she says with a twinkle in her eye.

"I was a rebellious teenager, so when I was fifteen, my mother thought I'd do better if I lived with my older sister and her husband. It was while I was with them that I had the accident."

Stella went swimming one day with some friends and her cousins. On their way back in an old jalopy, "the tie rod broke and we rolled over." Stella would never be the same. Her left arm had been severed at the shoulder. For the first and only time in her life, Stella fainted. When she awoke, still at the accident site, she remembers saying to herself, "This is a dream. I'm still dreaming. Things like this simply don't happen to people like us."

For months afterward, Stella remembers, she was angry at God. "I thought this was the most horrible thing imaginable. I wanted to die. If there was a God," I imagined, "he wouldn't let this happen to me." Now she can say about the same incident, "God's been chasing me for a long time. Back then, I didn't know he was hitting me over the head with a two-by-four to try to knock some spiritual sense into my life. The accident was the start of some direction in my life."

The state vocational rehabilitation unit sent Stella to the city for training. There she met her future husband, John. "Back then, I became determined to show that just because I had only one arm, I still could do what everyone else could. My mother used to tell me, 'What did one little old arm mean anyway? You still have a strong body.' " Stella exclaims with appreciation, "God has certainly blessed me — wow!"

John and Stella were married in 1954, much to the disappointment of John's family, who thought he was marrying beneath his station. John's was a proud family of Mexican descent who wanted their son to marry someone well-educated and more polished than Stella. But married they were, and the first of their four children came along the very next year. Stella calls John her guardian angel. She expresses gratitude to God in almost every sentence and is one of the most humble people one could ever encounter. Whenever someone compliments her on her perseverance or her light-heartedness, she simply retorts, "It's not me — it's God. He must be getting mighty tired though, because he's been carrying me for a long time!"

In 1981 Stella's life changed again. While showering, she noticed that the skin on her left breast, which had always looked chafed where she lost her arm, had split. That afternoon she was in the surgeon's office and heard him ask, "Why did you wait so long?"

Before the surgery that followed, the surgeon told her that if the lump wasn't cancerous, she would be out of the operating room in twenty minutes. If it was cancerous, the operation would take two hours. "The first thing I did upon awakening from surgery was look at the clock; four hours had passed. It was then that I knew for sure." They removed the breast and sixteen cancerous nodes. One year of chemotherapy followed.

As she lay in bed one morning four years later, Stella felt a pain in her neck and then "went stiff as a board." The cancer had metasticized (spread) to her spinal column and had invaded her central nervous system. Since then, her hips, both her legs, her shoulders, and her arm have been affected by the cancer. She has undergone several chemotherapy treatment series, the most recent lasting one solid year. Each bone site has been irradiated. Still, Stella lives on with the gaiety and joy of a schoolgirl.

Strangely enough, Stella can say today, "I have found such contentment and peace since my cancer diagnosis; I just wish everybody could have this kind of contentment and peace." She has no fear of death whatsoever. "If God wants me today, that's okay because I know he's waiting there for me with open arms." She has found tremendous peace in her spiritual life. She sees God in just about everything around her, especially in her husband, John. Hospitalization is a constant threat, if not from the cancer itself, then from the side effects of the treatment of the cancer. Yet she never complains. She prefers to see God's beauty all around her.

Day Twenty-one: Harmony

When decisions are made in harmony, they are in accord with a central principle or idea. All facets of the decision agree with one another. There is a pleasing or harmonious configuration of many pieces into one internally consistent whole. When something is in harmony, it is congruent with or agreeably related to a core homogenizing element. The many pieces coexist in an internal calmness or tranquillity, and each piece contributes measurably to the others.

The ideal of spiritual harmony can begin to emerge when we live in internal calmness, marvelously consistent with the will of God. Our actions and emotions are "in sync" or in concord with the central principle of God's love. We are living in a delightful symmetry with God's objectives and ways. We live in conformity with God's will in a positive and productively effective way. Harmony provides proportion, purpose, and possibility in our lives; we are in unison, in perfect alignment with peace and love. With harmony, there is order to our lives, and we know we are in communion with God.

❧

After her first treatment, Stella remembers agonizing, "Never again…I'll never go through another chemo treatment again!" Her doctors told her that it was her decision. After concentrated internal deliberation, she finally concluded, "It isn't my decision at all. I can't just throw my life away. If the Lord wants me to do it, then I have to." In this one statement, Stella had opted for harmony; she had aligned her will with the will of the Father as she understood it.

As Stella tells it, if she had refused further chemotherapy, she would have been like the faithful man who clung to the top of the church steeple during a flood. Three times rescuers tried to save him, but each time he rebuffed them, saying he preferred to let God save him. When the water rose even higher, he was swept away to his death. When he got to heaven, the man asked Saint Peter why God didn't help him. Saint Peter responded, "He tried three times, but you refused." Stella said, "I thought somehow that God was asking me to save my life, not for myself but for my family, and that the chemotherapy was the means he had provided for me to do just that. I had to do what I thought God wanted of me, no matter how uncomfortable it may be for me."

Everything about Stella speaks of a great internal calmness. Her speech, her movements, her peaceful attitude about the world, her complete lack of judging, and her loving confidence in the power of God. Asked to describe this calmness, she paused and said with her finger to her chin, "You just have to experience it; it's unexplainable." Her ordeal seems to have taken away her fears. "I don't worry about tomorrow or the bills or a clean floor. There was a time when I was a 'clean freak' but no more; many other things are much more important now.

"At times I can get out of harmony," Stella says. "This past year I was in the hospital three times. Over the Christmas holidays, my eldest daughter visited for the first time in three years. I wanted to share the holidays with her; I wanted to go shopping, out to lunch, and just spend time with her. I felt cheated that I couldn't. I also felt cheated because it was the first midnight Mass since John and I were married that I missed. I'm in the church choir and we had practiced long and hard for the midnight Mass presentation. I had to miss that, too. I was angry at God that I had to have cancer and be in the hospital. At first I thought that I was wrong to become angry, but then I thought that perhaps this anger did have a purpose after all. I prayed my way through it, and it did bring me into closer relationship with God after all." Being "in relationship" is perhaps the most dramatic reality of harmony in Stella's life.

Meditations on Harmony

MORNING

Harmony synthesizes me.

As I awaken, an ancient hate is passing from me and is replaced by harmony. This hate, of which I had been unaware, was simply a misperception, but it caused great turmoil in my soul. Harmony synthesizes the two sides of me; the part that is human and *of* the world and the spiritual side, which is only *in* the world. Harmony emerges when I can give my real self, my spiritual side, the leadership position in my life.

AFTERNOON

Harmony ends my senseless striving for more.

Harmony joins me with the grace of God. Harmony sets me on the journey toward God and ends my senseless striving for more on this plane. Harmony lets me realize fully that the past is gone and gives me the understanding not to preserve it in any way that might bind my spiritual development. Harmony allows me to connect my real self with the reality of God and detach from my sick body.

EVENING

My problems are absurd when seen with harmony.

Give my heart harmony, O God, so I can see that my choices are not difficult, because my problems are absurd when seen in your clear light. Harmony renders separation impossible, a mere relic of the past that is no longer useful to me. Let me rest tonight in harmony, knowing there is no division in heaven.

Day Twenty-Two: Patience

Patience implies toleration, but not necessarily meekness. Patience is persevering in the face of an identified obstacle or hardship; persisting even though adversity may present itself; enduring in a gentle, even kindly manner, unhurried but unremitting. Patience is the quality that enables us to bear frustration for the sake of a higher good. Patience is not hasty or impetuous, rather it is steadfast even when opposed by difficulty or adversity. Patience allows us to bear up under trials calmly and without complaint. One who is patient tolerates provocation and handles strain.

Spiritual patience enables us to postpone worldly or physical pleasures or impulses for the greater good of God's love. Demonstrations of irritability, anger, sorrow, self-embellishment, and other actions of the world self are transformed by patience into acts of love in service to the will of God. Patience places God's love in its many forms above the impetuous ways of the world. Patience transcends frantic excitement and discontent with the knowing understanding that all is right in Jesus. Patience trades the frenetic hurry of the world with the mysterious calm of the universe. Patience is profound and supernally deep; the world is shallow and shrill by comparison.

ॐ

"I can't say that I'm patient. In some ways, I've learned some patience, but I have a long way to go." Here is Stella's humility at work. I encouraged her to add more honesty to her humility. She said, "My illness has taught me patience in so many ways." One of the techniques for patience that she uses is a simple question. "When things get rough or when I'm startled, I simply ask myself, 'What would Christ do in a situation like this one?' " She relates with a confident puzzlement, "I guess when I really think about it, all the events of my life have taught me a bit more patience."

Two years ago, Stella's son, Paul, was the victim of a tragic accident that left him brain damaged. He lives with Stella and John and their youngest child, Jodie. Paul is confined to a wheelchair and has a very difficult time speaking clearly. "I've learned a lot of patience through this ordeal. But God is good and has shown me the way to endure. We all love Paul very much, as we do all our children. We'd do anything for him. I could certainly use more patience with Paul."

Stella not only endures, she thrives with a sense of internal calm that touches your heart. "Right now, I'm not impatient; I really feel the peace of the universe within me. There was a time, though, when I was impatient. When I was a young mother, I felt so pressured. But now I can see the true reality of my purpose on this earth. God is so good to me."

Meditations on Patience

MORNING

I see the blessing my sickness can be for me.

In the brightness of the dawn, I realize that my disease is not an attack on me. I see it more clearly now, holy Friend. I see the blessing my sickness can be for me. Grant me the patience today to wait in peace for the blessings of my sickness to be revealed to me.

AFTERNOON

What would Christ do in this situation?

Patience produces results. Patience lets me take a step back and ask, "What would Christ do in this situation?" The answer to this question will always come when patience is present, and the patient answer will always bring me peace. I am not mandated to react to this world; I can merely respond with pearls of patience and open my arms to receive the perfection of God that cannot be denied.

EVENING

Divine Healer, direct my dreams.

I drift into your infinite patience as I close my eyes tonight. I am held in your hand, and I rest more deeply than ever before. Patience never attacks. Therefore, I need not fear; patience is love and so am I, so I am always safe. I cannot be attacked. Divine Healer, direct my dreams this night and help me know again what I knew before but somehow forgot.

Day Twenty-Three: Strength

More than anything else, to have strength means to have potency, the ability to do things. A strong person can perform a great deal. Strength implies a certain toughness, an ability to resist attack. Strength has the power to withstand considerable force; it has a capacity for sustained exertion. To be strong is to be firm, robust, and vital. The virtue of strength makes us impregnable to invasion and vigorous in defense. Strength has stamina, nerve, and muscle.

Spiritual strength is omnipotent; it can do anything and resist anything. When we are spiritually strong, there is no need to attack; when we have strength, we can be at peace. The strong person does not need enemies; those who think they can be hurt do not possess strength. Illness cannot hurt our real spiritual selves; therefore, the degree to which we believe ourselves to be spiritually impregnable is the degree to which we possess strength. The strong person is straightforward and upright; deceit and underhanded treachery are alien characteristics to those who are strong.

"Boy, I've got determination; I'm much stronger than I was last week," Stella announces with a fixed chin. One gets the impression that she has said the same thing every week for the past ten years. Strength is a virtue with which Stella seems well endowed.

"God is my strength," she says. "He gives me what I need to resist all my problems and cares. Losing my arm was a training for me so I could be strong with my cancer. The same determination I had with my arm I can now call upon. It's not my strength; it's God's. My strength truly lies in the fact that I don't have to defend anything anymore. I'm defenseless and I'm strong. Knowing that I am protected by God's strength gives me great peace of mind."

Stella clearly knows that she can tap into God's strength through prayer. "I pray a lot. I ask God to cure me. I know he will do what's right for me; anything is possible with God." She talks about the will to live and the will to love. "Cancer can't touch or hurt my love for God, for life, the joy of going to Mass when I can, even the joy of taking a ride to the post office." But her prayer doesn't center on her illness. Her prayer is obviously a marvelously uplifting experience for her. "I can't imagine anyone praying and dwelling on an illness. I ask God to heal me if it is his will, but mainly

I pray to feel good and not feel bad. Why dwell on your sickness? Think of God's beauty and bounty."

Finally, Stella's strength is captured in the courage she shows in enduring the seemingly endless chemotherapy treatments. "It takes a lot of courage to go to chemo. Even now, when I know what to expect and generally how to handle it best for me, it's still very difficult to go to my treatments. The other day it was snowing and I was hoping in my heart that it would be too icy for me to go get my treatment." She laughs at herself as she realizes how much of herself she has just exposed. Nonetheless, she seems to enjoy the seeming paradox between her courage and her self-revelation.

Meditations on Strength

MORNING

I need your strength to get through this day.

Divine Physician, let me go to your altar of strength. I have no strength but from you. But you deprive me of nothing, and I need your strength to get through this day. Healing can be hard work; I step aside to let you lead me where I need to go. I must exert myself constantly. Make your strength, Lord, the foundation of my stamina today.

AFTERNOON

Your strength creates security in me all day.

I find your strength in me when my mind is unified, not split, when I am at peace and need not attack or feel attacked. Your strength creates security in me all day. I know your strength lies within me; I need only tap into it through prayer. Today let me choose a learning path that teaches me strength. Strength accumulates in me when I'm at peace. When I'm at war, I am depleted.

EVENING

My rationale for choice is simple.

Let me rest my head, knowing that conflict is brought to peace. My rationale for choice is simple: my strength is your love, so I will continuously choose love. Divine Teacher, yours is a curriculum of joy, power, and strength. I need to learn the paradox that when I am defenseless, I have strength; when I think I'm powerful, I'm actually weak. Help me, Lord, learn this lesson as I dream tonight.

Day Twenty-Four: Transcendence

Transcendence means going beyond, going over into another dimension. To be transcendent is to exceed the normal limits of ordinary expectations. Transcendence implies that something out of the norm has occurred. Something has been more than surpassed. Transcendence means that another dimension has been achieved — a dimension that was formerly beyond comprehension. To transcend is to move out of this world and enter another.

The spiritual ideal of transcendence, of course, is growing from the worldly level to the level of the Spirit. When we cross this supernatural barrier, we do more than enter a new dimension, more than simply exceed the world or outstrip the earth and its constraints. Indeed, we become transformed as we move into this new paradigm, and our fundamental composition and character are changed. When we are transformed, we are dramatically altered in potential; we are converted. Spiritual transcendence implies that a core shift in meaning and purpose, in direction and goal, has emerged; the physical has been transfigured into the spiritual. To be transformed is to find true reality.

Stella has given herself a new perspective on life in general and a new way of looking at her existence. She consistently reminds herself that she is but "a little speck of sand." Since being stricken with cancer, Stella has developed a deeper and deeper appreciation for life, for the beauty of the earth, and for all people around her. "Everything seems more awesome," she relates. "I'm more grateful; I can't believe that God continues to shower his grace upon me and my family.

"My illness has transformed me. I'm intensely aware and much more sensitive. A ride in the country is a blessing for me." Certainly, Stella exists on this earthly plane; but somehow she also lives simultaneously on the plane of heaven. She is physically here but also strangely not.

I had the thought when speaking with Stella that what she considers to be obvious and self-evident would be profound for the rest of us. For example, last winter Stella fell on the sidewalk and broke her hip and her collarbone. This led to more surgery and a long physical therapy. She says, "At physical therapy, they all bragged about me, telling me what a fighter I was. They praised me all the time and used me as a model for the other patients. They said, 'You have amazed us!' But their praise is misplaced. I'm just doing what God wants. It's not me doing all that; it's God."

Stella's husband, John, is with her through all this. He relates, "She has found the true reality. She knows where life and love come from. Stella knows the source of her strength. She has a vision of all this that is not of this world. The things that have happened to us have served to shape us into what we are today. Sometimes it is scary when you really think of God so close to us all the time. He's here right now."

Meditations on Transcendence

MORNING

Help me leave the world behind.

Abba, let me awaken to the truth. Let me no longer see what isn't there and choose only to see your true reality. Let me make room in my heart and mind for your truth, beauty, and goodness. Help me to leave the world behind. At the same time, I am in this world but also beyond it. Here is a place where I can find peace.

AFTERNOON

I withhold no one and nothing from your peace.

Let me not look upon the errors my brothers and sisters may have made in the past. The past is gone, and the errors don't matter. Errors aren't real; only love is real. Abba, help me focus on love today. I am a love-finder today for your sake as well as mine and the world's. In helping me do this, you are constantly on my mind. I extend your love through forgiveness, spreading your peace to all. I withhold no one and nothing from your peace.

EVENING

I paint pictures of peace in my dreams tonight.

Without forgiveness, the true reality of my brothers and sisters lies asleep as I toss and turn. The picture I had of them in the past means nothing. I paint pictures of peace in my dreams tonight using a paintbrush called forgiveness. I rest in sublime solace knowing I have decided to allow my inner teacher to instruct me. You are the source and center of my life, Lord. I choose to give myself back to you.

Day Twenty-five: Self-discipline

Self-discipline is the imposing of order upon ourselves for the purpose of training for something new or correcting something that requires adjustment. Self-discipline gives us control over ourselves and molds or perfects our physical, mental, and moral character. We can achieve more, be more productive, when we are self-disciplined. Self-discipline implies enforcing obedience from one part of ourselves onto another; it allows us to develop in a way that would have been impossible before. Self-discipline usually includes training and drill, practice, and on the strictly worldly level, even repression or punishment.

Spiritual self-discipline places value on the spiritual self over the worldly self as its primary goal. When Saint Paul remarked that he always finds himself doing the things he doesn't want to do, he was making reference to the necessity of spiritual self-discipline. He wanted the spirit self to have supremacy over the worldly self. As we become accustomed to new attitudes, skills, competencies, or beliefs, we achieve self-discipline. Spiritual self-discipline is required of us as we continuously discover the central purpose and true reality of our existence.

和

"It takes a great deal of self-discipline to carry on. But I can't give up, because God is so good to me. He won't let me give up; he'll hit me with a two-by-four again," Stella relates. "I fall short lots of times. But God gave me two legs and a mind, and I must use them all to serve him."

Stella seems to have given God that total "Yes" mentioned earlier. She claims to have accepted fully the love of God, and she follows his ways with all her being. Her core belief is "I don't deserve credit for what I do." Her constant prayer is "How great thou art!"

"With a giving husband like John, I could constantly say things like 'John, would you get me a glass of ice water?' But what would that accomplish? I need to do things myself, even though my pain is with me. I need to exercise my body and my self-discipline at the same time.

"If I felt a little under the weather, I could ask my beautiful daughter Jodie to prepare dinner for us. Sometimes I have to push myself to get up to fix supper or to do the dishes." When Stella's stamina is low, her self-discipline seems to take over. "I must constantly say to myself, 'You're strong enough to do it yourself.' I'm in constant conversation with God."

Meditations on Self-discipline

MORNING

I am dependent upon you alone, Lord.

By choosing your lead, Abba, I provide an opportunity for my own healing. When I look through Christ's eyes today, I see only the real world, not some fake, frightening world that I myself have made. That's not the world I choose today. I am dependent upon you alone, Lord. Let me exercise whatever self-discipline I require today to join myself steadfastly to you.

AFTERNOON

I am part of the grain of your love.

When I experience discomfort, let my self-discipline be aroused so I may do what is necessary to correct the problem. I am not alien to you — I am your child. I cannot be dissociated from you; I am part of the grain of your love. Let me not forget how powerful I am with you and that anything is possible for you. Let me discipline myself to accept your will, whatever it may be today. I know healing is taking place somehow.

EVENING

I am in no doubt about your work in my life.

I am not divided from you, Abba. I am in no doubt about your work in my life. You speak to me constantly. Give me the discipline to listen to your whispers of faith, your songs of joy, and your poems of truth. As I dream your dreams tonight, I can listen to your guidance and be glad that I chose your way, not mine; your words, not mine; your perspective, not mine. Good night.

Decision Prayer

Living Presence, today let me truly know and understand that the power of decision is my own. I know it is your will that I accept fully what you created me to be. Let me be humble in acknowledging my inheritance of mightiness. I will no longer hold myself prisoner. I wish to be free. Every temptation to anger is actually an opportunity to find freedom as I decide to choose love instead of fear. When I forgive those I thought trespassed against me, I see that they are actually one with me.

Lord, I seek release from the chains that bind me to this world. Let me devote today in profound solitude to my search so I may join with you to make my decisions your decisions. I am incomplete without you; I am made whole and holy when I am with you. You have given me so many gifts; let me honor your gift of free will so I can make decisions about my sickness with conscious intent. Let me take your hand, Lord, and walk with you today. Allow me to make my will your will. Let me practice daily, for faith develops from practice, and truth comes from understanding the meaning you give to my life. Let me share your will and your purpose for me. Amen.

Chapter Seven

ACTION

Patients must develop a personal commitment to becoming experts in their own disease. They need to gather enough courage to accept their own mortality while deciding to live their life to the fullest right now.

Introduction

You need more than the first five functions of the personality as outlined in Chapters Two through Six to achieve the spiritual growth from your sickness that can be rightfully and joyfully yours. In addition to these first five, you need to use the sixth function of the personality, action. Our God is a God of action, and it is through action that every great success is accomplished. Action is what produces results. You can learn how to take effective action with your sickness. Action is a gift that you can give to yourself.

Anthony Robbins describes action as a cause set into motion. To have a cause, you must make a decision. If you wish to be holy, if you wish to engage your life in the true reality and be led by your spiritual self, then you must change your physical and mental actions to match the state of spiritual unity you desire.

First, you must ask yourself, "What is my cause in life?" Is it spiritual wholeness? To go into the Father's house? Perhaps it is healing. The second question is "What are the actions that can set my cause into motion?" Think about all the things you have kept from the Holy Spirit, saving them to settle by yourself. Has it ever occurred to you that it is these same things that kept you apart from healing?

To move beyond your illness, you need to give all of yourself — every bit — to the Spirit, who knows how to look upon your cares so they will disappear. Develop the ways of the Holy Spirit — to look on everything as another step toward the wholeness of God.

In each day and in each hour, spend time with God, and always try to give forgiveness everywhere you can. Your forgiveness lights your world and brings healing to you. God will take the final giant step for you, but you must take the thousand tiny steps toward God.

Offer thanks that in God everything, even your sickness, will find its freedom. In your gratitude, escape the pain of illness and find healing. Don't try to compare yourself with the sick, the weak, the needy, or the fearful. When you do that, you risk being cut off from the unity of creation and the healing power within you. When you identify with sickness or weakness, you will be drawn to become like them. Gratitude goes hand in hand with love and with strength: where one is, you will find the other.

Whenever you judge, blame, or criticize, you will always bring pain; your attack will always boomerang. Attack, in any form, will bring you distress.

The thought that you can somehow enhance yourself through self-righteousness or self-aggrandizement will only nail you to your own cross of deceit and pain.

Another action that can transform your sickness into a learning experience is acceptance. Acceptance is action; it is creative work that can bring the power of the universe to you. You can forge your life into an interlocking chain of acceptance and forgiveness by

- truly owning that you are a child of God
- remembering always that you are not a body
- adopting love as your only cause
- affirming forgiveness as your one function

Dr. Bernie Siegel encourages his patients to find life and love in their illnesses. He maintains that through this process each person will find the path to his or her own healing. Patients must develop a personal commitment to becoming experts in their own disease. They need to gather enough courage to accept their own mortality while deciding to live their life to the fullest right now. As a physician, he recommends that his patients take these actions: Refuse to act like a patient. Learn how to hope and pray. Develop peace of mind. Listen to their inner voice. Meditate. Relax. Communicate with their inner voice.

Lorraine's Story

In January 1986, Lorraine, then aged forty-three, noticed strange sensations in her leg muscles. "What could this be?" she wondered. For the next year, the feelings would come and go. Sometimes they would become intense, while at other times they would subside to nothing at all. Several doctors and eighteen months later, Lorraine was diagnosed with multiple sclerosis, or MS, after an MRI (magnetic resonance imaging) test. She already had educated herself about MS, since one of her doctors had mentioned it as a possible diagnosis some months before. Not only that, by a strange coincidence, her mother-in-law had suffered from MS for many years.

It was on a Friday when Lorraine was finally diagnosed. She went home to her husband, Bob, and their three daughters, then aged twenty-two, twenty-one, and eighteen, and spent the entire night alternately crying, thinking, and praying. She waited to see the sunrise and to seek, as she termed it, "the illumination and light of the Eucharist." She felt rooted in the Eucharist, and during that first Mass after her diagnosis, she prayed with all her might that she might be spared this terrible malady. She told God, "I don't want to do this!" Then, at the eucharistic prayer in response to "Let us give thanks to the Lord our God," she blurted out without realizing what she was saying, "It is hard (instead of 'right') to give him thanks and praise."

At first, the denial was pervasive for Lorraine. For another year, she would burst into tears at the thought of MS. Others would say to her, "You can't have MS; you're too nice a person…you're like a saint!" She could only react with fear, remembering the suffering her mother-in-law had endured. Lorraine resisted at every turn, wanting, even demanding, that this "cup be taken from me."

The memory of her mother-in-law haunted Lorraine's being. As a caregiver, she had spent hours just listening to her mother-in-law's stories and the lament of a woman who felt much had been taken from her. MS had left her mother-in-law with her life but had stripped her of everything else.

Lorraine was filled with empathy and pity that she couldn't do more for the older woman. She felt helpless at times, always desiring that she could find some miracle to lessen the sting of the dreaded disease her mother-in-law had contracted. Now it was Lorraine's turn to feel the pain and walk the walk. How would she do it?

Lorraine's marriage was good. Her daughters were perfect pictures of health and beauty to her. She had lived vigorously and vibrantly. "Is all this to be taken from me?" she mused. She and her husband had long talks seeking answers to how his family had dealt with his mother's MS. What she found was that Bob's father had virtually taken over the family. He wanted his wife's illness to have as little impact on the children as possible. So Bob had little memory of any coping styles or suggestions for Lorraine about how to handle all this. Bob's father didn't allow the kids to have an active part in their mom's illness; he protected them.

Lorraine then looked to her own family of origin for guidance. She had had a life-giving relationship with her father, a professional musician. "He was a special man," related Lorraine. "Everybody loved him." She remembers his personal philosophy of living well. "How often," she recalls, "I heard him say, 'Everything happens for the best' and 'If you had a million bucks, you could never live better than this!' " Her relationship with her dad sculpted Lorraine's image of God. For her, God is a big benevolent Father into whose arms she could crawl like a small girl and nestle in the peace and strength of the universe in perfect security.

Gradually, Lorraine began to climb out of the pit of despair she had dug for herself. She began to see a flicker of the light of hope that had grown so dim since her diagnosis. She prayed now with a peace that began to surpass the peace she had experienced before the trauma of MS. Something was changing for her, something she could not explain but — something, nonetheless — with the power of the universe behind it. How could this be happening? How did Lorraine transform her tragedy into a lesson for peace? What was her secret?

Day Twenty-six: Honesty

Persons of honesty are seekers of God's truth, beauty, and goodness in everything. They transcend mere honesty and grow instead toward the lofty heights of emotional and spiritual honesty. They are incapable of being dishonest, either with their brothers and sisters or with themselves. They see God's hand in all things. Honest persons are fair and straightforward in their conduct, their adherence to the facts, and their sincerity. For them, the primary fact of their existence — the one around which all other facts revolve — is God's presence within them. This fact they find indisputable; it serves as the fulcrum of their lives.

People who practice the healing virtue of honesty possess honor and integrity. They are not fragmented; they are whole and unified in thought and emotion. They are free from any internal fraud or deception. They are genuine, frank, and real, entertaining no illusions. Their purpose in life is aligned with God's purpose for them; they do let trivial goals clutter their lives. They are true to the central purpose they continuously pursue. They tolerate no lie, falsehood, or error within themselves. They regularly transcend this world through prayer and meditation, preferring the internal peace and serenity of their spiritual reality. They seek to become one, in accord with this reality rather than the world's. They are authentic, certain, solid, and undisguised in who and what they are.

❧

Lorraine's illness allowed her truth and beauty to emerge even more clearly than it had before. As she reflects upon the year following her diagnosis, she can see how the illusion of fear gripped her mind and distorted her thinking. Now, she relates, "I'm convinced that the biggest part of my fear was my failure to look at my illness from the perspective of right now and to know that God would certainly provide all the grace I needed to face it with him." Lorraine credits this bedrock honesty with changing her heart and allowing her to eventually accept her MS and to say "Yes" to God.

Acceptance is one of the most significant healing actions of honesty. Through prayer, study, and being with God all through the day, Lorraine was able to achieve balance in her life and to accept her MS as a fact of her existence the same as having brown eyes and brown hair. The beauty and honesty in this realization enabled her to accept her MS as merely an intrusion into her life that she didn't invite but that she doesn't "have to feed; but... needs to own, just like I own that I'm five feet two." Through honest acceptance, Lorraine moved from the turmoil-producing position of "I don't see anything good here, and I don't want to do this thing called MS!" to the realization that "God's final chapter has already been written, eternity is now, everything will be okay."

Because of her mother-in-law's experience, Lorraine's fear of MS was initially even more fear-producing than it might have otherwise been. "I did a lot of crying in those first months," she remembers. "But sooner or later I came face to face with the thing I feared the most — MS. This confrontation gave me freedom.

"Honesty gave me the insight to see that, while I didn't have to want MS, I could work through the processes of grief, denial, sadness, and confusion and emerge even better than I had been. I smashed against the wall of truth about my MS, and confusion was my bounce off that wall. The action of grieving gave me the freedom that I longed for." Lorraine goes on to explain that it's a new kind of freedom, a freedom based on the absolute reality that God's grace will always be there for her.

Meditations on Honesty

MORNING

Truth needs no defense.

Today I will act only in truth. I will not see what isn't there; I will not believe what isn't true. Truth is evident, and I accept it as complete. I will make room for truth and drain myself of attack and condemnation. Healing flourishes in truth but shrivels in attack. The world can work against truth, but truth simply is. Truth needs no defense.

AFTERNOON

I will not stumble now.

In honesty, I will not wish to be somewhere else. I am here in truth; therefore, here is where I am supposed to be. Truth goes beyond the beliefs of this world; it can appear strange to me, yet I am called to perceive in truth. I will not stumble now. Truth is in me, and I am delighted to look at it.

EVENING

Truth is God's will.

Truth dawns on me. I bring myself to the altar of truth today, and in my brokenness I see the brilliant radiance that lies within. I cannot deny the truth in me; it cannot be explained but it can be experienced. Truth overcomes error and gives the solace of knowing that all things are unfolding as they should. Truth is not fragile. It is tough; it is God's will.

Day Twenty-seven: Inspiration

Perhaps the word *inspiration* suggests choirs of celestial power descending and taking over your soul. It sounds too lofty, too sublime, for mere mortals to attain. Yet we *are* called to it. Inspiration is actually quite action oriented. It means to be infused with light and life, to be influenced, guided, or moved by the Divine. It means to be spurred on, to communicate with the cosmic reality, to produce something outstanding or brilliant. Inspiration means to stimulate, animate, or enliven. It's the action of moving or illuminating the intellect or the emotions. Inspiration is an action in itself. When a person is inspired, some shift from the human to the superhuman has occurred, some basic core has been touched that releases the true strength of God's healing power. To be inspired is to fully recognize the true nature of the self and the mighty mechanisms of care deep inside.

≈

Lorraine's image of God as her ultimate security provided her with the "inspiration connection" she needed to find her true self and live in her world with MS. "My mother-in-law is now in the communion of saints and is, at this very moment, cheering for me and my family," Lorraine came to realize. "I have immense gratitude for her because she taught me so much." Such inspiration, such enlightenment, could only come from one Source.

Lorraine expressed the virtue of inspiration in action with these words: "I don't give my MS room. I don't welcome it as a visitor, nor do I fight it as though it were an enemy. We all fear the unknown. We fear because we have yet to genuinely face the real problem. The problem is not the MS; the problem is how we respond to it."

Inspiration is a free gift from God, although its development can be facilitated through prayer and contemplation. The benefits it produces for you in practical terms are legion. Lorraine explains that some people are so afraid of contracting a disease themselves that they try to find an explanation as to why you got what you did. "When I explain that I have MS, some people jump to conclusions such as 'You must have MS because you didn't sleep enough or you ate too much candy or you didn't get enough exercise or you inherited it.' They need to search for an explanation because they are unconsciously trying to insulate themselves from you so they don't become vulnerable to it themselves. Indeed, sometimes even I erroneously think that perhaps I neglected this precious gift of my body that once was whole and wonderful."

Realizing that they are speaking out of their own fear, Lorraine attempts to view "naysayers" with love. From the stance of love, she can say, "What they're saying doesn't mean a darned thing! They're blinded by fear that they might wind up the same way. I feel I have a license to feel better, and I try to do just that each and every day."

Meditations on Inspiration

MORNING

Inspiration helps me abandon any thoughts of death and despair.

I am infused with universal inspiration from the Holy Spirit. The right thoughts I think today move me to actions of love. Inspiration helps me abandon any thoughts of death and despair, replacing them with brightness and joy. As I rest, I am inspired. As inspiration fills me, I am healed. Inspiration changes me from chaos to order. Inspiration cannot be deceived.

AFTERNOON

I am an inspired child of God; I do not fear.

Today I withdraw all value and all energy from that which gives me pain; I invest this newly inspired energy into that which extends love. I look directly at my sickness and see it clearly, realizing that it has no power to harm me. I am an inspired child of God; I do not fear.

EVENING

Inspiration brings power.

My inspiration comes from a force the world has no power to resist. This evening I forgive myself for any and all transgressions and permit inspiration to fill those spaces in me that need healing. Where there was suffering, there is now joy; where there was sickness, healing lies. Death is replaced by life and pain with delight. Inspiration brings power.

Day Twenty-eight: Kindness

The healing virtue of kindness requires that we be gentle toward ourselves and our bodies in every way possible. It means to give care, to accept our bodies as a gift from God and as the central means of communication with others. Kindness implies being affectionate and loving, giving pleasure or relief to ourselves. It means acting in a gracious manner, with courteous gestures of goodwill to ourselves and others. To be kind means to be tender, sympathetic, mild, friendly, and helpful. Kindness is soothing, tolerant, considerate, and positively docile. The opposite of kindness is violence, interruption, discourtesy.

Before she contracted MS, Lorraine had always prided herself on living to the fullest. Her immediate reaction to the MS was to refuse to face it until she absolutely had to. Once she realized God had given her the grace to face it, she again began to think that she could live her life to the fullest.

"To help myself do this," she says, "I would touch and even caress my own body to bring a sense of relief. I would talk to my disease, telling it that I knew it had to survive but that I needed to get on with my life. I never tried to kill the disease. I was gentle with everything. Certainly, I would rather the MS went away. But I knew this wasn't possible, so I took very good care of it and of me."

Lorraine developed an awe of her own body. She looks at the twitching muscles in her arm and says, "Poor little arm. I want to help you and ease your pain in any way that I can." Miraculously, she says, "...the pain lessens a lot."

Meditations on Kindness

MORNING

Kindness lets me lower all the barriers.

Today I offer total kindness and I am healed completely. I walk in peace, following the road called kindness. My mind is healed by kindness. My mind was formerly split, but kindness welds it into a whole. Kindness lets me lower all the barriers and offer my true self to all God's children.

AFTERNOON

Kindness transforms my world from chaos to peace.

Kindness sets things right for me. As I peer out my window, I see a new light and a new day. When I find ways to demonstrate kindness, the world changes from madness to peace. Kindness frees me to be strong, because every action of kindness brings me closer to God. Kindness brings my love out in the open and fills me with security.

EVENING

Kindness unites me with God's children.

Through kindness, I can escape the misery of this sickness. I am motivated to act in kindness by love, which in turn showers me with God's healing power. Kindness helps me remember my purpose here as I am made whole. Kindness unites me with God's children and allows me to see all events as opportunities for healing.

Day Twenty-nine: Steadfastness

To be steadfast is to be fixed in place, to be immovable and not subject to change. It means to be faithful, firm in belief, determined, loyal and adherent to a set of guiding values and principles. The steadfast person is direct and sure in movement, unfaltering, and acts with little variation. Such a person's feelings and thoughts are constant, purposeful, and attached to a belief system. He or she is dependable and steady, unswerving and staunch, resolute and principled.

Lorraine claims that her certainty comes from her sense of personal balance. "My secret of life is my balance. I try to inject balance into whatever I'm doing, because when things are out of balance, they quickly move into chaos. To be steadfast is to live in God's holy *now.*" When she exercises steadfastness, Lorraine reminds us that it "is not a panacea in itself, but it can make the way for peace of mind and tills the soil of my soul so it can become fruitful for me." She likes to remember that the "Holy Spirit has never given up on me; how could I do that to him?"

The strain of living in constant pain can be almost intolerable. However, through steadfastness it is possible to enlist heavenly powers in the struggle to get through the day. Of course, steadfastness in itself is not the goal; it is simply one of the vehicles to utilize toward the goal. But what a mighty vehicle it is!

Meditations on Steadfastness

MORNING

I have the will to love.

The Holy Spirit offers me the gifts of permanence and unshakable determination. The fortress of my love for God withstands any onslaught the world may have to launch. The spirit in me is perfect and therefore unchangeable. Above the will to live, I have the will to love. And all healing involves placing love where fear once was.

AFTERNOON

My will leads me toward healing in steadfast love.

My rest comes from my spiritual awakening. As I recognize my true will to love, I become steadfast in desiring that God's will be done. As I grow in steadfastness, I am more convinced that my will and God's will are converging. My will is empowered by God's and guides me toward healing in steadfast love.

EVENING

Let me hold fast to a real sense of my genuine being.

Lord God, give me steadfastness to act in accordance with my most sacred beliefs. Let me hold fast to a real sense of my genuine and fundamental being. I experience no doubts when I am steadfast in your love. I know that you have shared your being with me, Lord, and that you have absolute confidence in my outcome.

Day Thirty: Perseverance

Perseverance is characterized by persistence. In spite of any influences to the contrary, the persevering person plods on in whatever undertaking or cause he or she has adopted. Perseverance is embedded in continuance, permanence, firmness, and stability. It adheres to singleness of purpose and patience, tenacity and constancy. People who persevere have stamina, backbone, courage, grit. They endure; they're indefatigable. Patients with perseverance can carry on in the face of adversity; they take action that they would not be up to without the healing virtue of perseverance.

Perseverance incorporates the best of the other virtues, because it can inspire us to proceed when little hope is left, to have mercy when compassion seems withered, to have gratitude when we might want to wail and lament, to be humorous when gravity seems more appropriate. In short, the healing virtue of perseverance allows us to run that extra mile when the storm is raging and the darkness seems smothering. Perseverance brings the light of Christ as the Holy Spirit did to the upper room on the first Pentecost, when all appeared foreboding and bleak. The Holy Spirit carries the gifts of the healing virtues on the wings of perseverance.

How do you develop the marvelous virtue of perseverance, especially when sickness is robbing you of the very strength to carry on at all, much less persevere? Lorraine's attitude is one of "soaking in the abundant present, because this time will never come again."

For Lorraine, perseverance means surrender to Jesus in the spiritual sense outlined in the Serenity Prayer espoused by Alcoholics Anonymous. She says, "Even though I may be dying inside, even though I may be petrified by my MS, I know that I will carry on as long as God's grace keeps sustaining me; and that will never stop." How much strength, beauty, and perseverance can you see in this statement of Lorraine's? "MS is like a flat tire. It's a real pain, but it doesn't have to ruin your trip; your destination remains the same." Perseverance brings its own gifts. As with all virtues, practicing one enhances the practice of others.

Lorraine says she has learned to develop gratitude by paying attention to perseverance. "I get up every day and sing 'It's a beautiful morning.' I'm never quite sure what the day will bring, but whatever it is, I know that I'll be ready for it." Before her sickness, she took things for granted. "I believed that everything should go according to my own plan; I was a recovering perfectionist. I would work long and hard, do anything to see that the job got accomplished. Now I realize that accomplishment doesn't matter. What matters is perseverance — doing the best I can with the available light and being grateful for what I am able to do."

Meditations on Perseverance

MORNING

Help me focus on your abundance, Lord.

It is indeed true that all my prayers are answered. In this harsh morning light, though, I'm tempted to believe that my prayers end in failure. Help me, Lord, to continuously recognize what I already have. Help me focus on your abundance and persistently turn away from silly thoughts of lack or scarcity. Grant me the perseverance I need to pray constantly for peace and love.

AFTERNOON

God, you are my remedy.

Prayer is my ultimate action, and prayer of forgiveness is the most meaningful kind. Prayer keeps me united with you. Prayer is the medium of communication that frees me from the bondage of this world. I persevere in my belief that I will be made whole. God, you are my remedy.

EVENING

I persevere in my dedication to you.

I surrender all to you, loving God; I let go in absolute faith. I persevere in my dedication to you. Your love surrounds me always. As I awaken into your life of bounty, I have no need for any form of expression that looks like sickness. I have but one God, and I persevere with you. I have banished all other gods as simple misperceptions on my part.

Action Prayer

Lord, my feet have reached the beautiful lawns that surround heaven's gate. Let me grow beyond anxiety, depression, and guilt. Let me accept the world, releasing it from my false expectations. Allow me to let go of the future; I know it is in your hands. I have no control over it, except to express my powerlessness. As I escape all fear of future pain, I find my way to peace in the present, certain of care the world cannot provide. Let me hear the song of heaven and the voice of Christ as I release the world, for it provides me with no safety. It is rooted in attack; all its "gifts" are but deceptions.

Help me, loving God, release my defensiveness and align my true self with your defenselessness, where my true strength resides. Loosen the iron grip that the need to attack has upon my heart. Give me your grace and the gifts of truth — inspiration, kindness, steadfastness, and perseverance. Finally, give me the courage and strength to act as you would have me act, in love and peace, with your Son as my model and your Spirit as my guide. I give you my life, Lord, forever. Amen.

Chapter Eight

TEN TECHNIQUES TO ACHIEVE HEALING

The restorative power of God is an awesome force for healing that lies within each of us. Fortunately, various techniques are available to help stimulate it.

- Education
- Relaxation
- Meditation
- Prayer
- Imagination and Fantasy
- Storytelling
- Drawings
- Reminiscing
- Sentence Completion
- Support Groups

The advent of sickness is a traumatic event in anyone's life. Grave, chronic — and especially terminal — conditions disturb our lives and alter our image of the world, of ourselves, and of God. Even in the best of situations, in which sufficient familial support, adequate financial resources, the availability of caregivers, and the presence of an intact self-esteem are all "in place," patients can still stumble and falter emotionally. When these ideal conditions are not present, psychic disturbances and mental breakdown can emerge, causing even greater turmoil. This book is predicated on the simple belief that healing is not of this world and that a keen awareness of God's presence within is essential for healing, regardless of the physical condition.

The restorative power of God is an awesome force for healing that lies within each of us. Fortunately, various techniques are available to help stimulate it. In this section, I've enumerated the most effective techniques that you can use profitably in your journey toward healing.

These techniques can be used individually, but their effectiveness is enhanced dramatically when practiced in a group. A group gives you the opportunity to share your innermost thoughts, ideas, secrets, doubts, fears, and joys in a facilitative, knowledgeable, and compassionate setting. Research studies repeatedly have found that those who can share themselves most openly are the ones who find the greatest levels of emotional wellness in their lives. This simple truth is the foundation of group dynamics and is the reason why "healing virtues groups" can be so filled with power. Here are the ten techniques.

Education

Everyone has heard that knowledge is power; healing is no exception. We need to educate ourselves in the processes and procedures of healing. This book provides a comprehensive educational program in two important areas. The first is the Motivational Model itself, graphically portrayed on page 22. The structure helps you understand how the personality works and demonstrates how you can change the functions of your personality. These six functions — believing, perceiving, thinking, feeling, deciding, and acting — together form the full range of psychological processes that allows us to take the path toward greater personal power, enhanced self-esteem, better interpersonal relations, health, and wholeness. But these six alone would prove insufficient for the task of healing without the cornerstone, the center of the process given to God. Without God, we can experience no genuine healing.

The second educational tool for healing introduced in this book is the use of the thirty healing virtues. Virtues are pieces of God-given application on the earthly plane. Virtues give us goals to follow, ideals to stretch toward, and targets to shoot for. The wellness model gives us the skeleton of healing and the thirty healing virtues flesh it out to create a fully formed whole. Here we have a powerful educational program, a unified curriculum of spiritual development, that can guide us faithfully along the healing path. It gives us structure and support. It provides a road map as well as a vehicle. It gives us all the equipment we need to travel the highway of healing and arrive safe and whole at the other end.

Relaxation

Relaxation, practiced in almost any form, produces therapeutic effects. The benefits of relaxation in the treatment of just about every known physical and emotional malady have been thoroughly documented. Relaxation is an almost foolproof procedure that pays handsome dividends.

There are many ways by which you can achieve a relaxed state, but perhaps the most common and easiest to use is progressive deep muscle relaxation. Relaxation is the first step toward your inner teacher in that it allows you to begin to focus within yourself, thereby shutting out the hectic, frantic, condemning world. Here is the starting point toward peace. The road toward spiritual and emotional solace begins through a gate called relaxation.

The following relaxation method has proven beneficial for my patients.

- Find a quiet, comfortable spot where you can be alone.
- Close your eyes and focus first on the muscles of your scalp. Progress gradually downward to your toes.
- In your mind's eye, picture each muscle group and "see" the muscles relaxing, loosening, and lengthening until they become smooth, limp, and drained of all the tension, pressure, and nervousness that was there. Imagine a soothing balm or ointment

being massaged into your muscles from the inside. Spend about one minute with each of these muscle areas in this order: (1) scalp, (2) face, (3) back of the neck, (4) shoulders and arms, (5) chest and abdomen, (6) back and lower back, (7) waist and buttocks, (8) thighs, (9) shins and calves, and (10) feet and toes.

- You may want to say a word such as *peace, calm,* or *rest* as you picture your muscles relaxing.

Learning to relax is a skill, like typing or driving or baking. Once you master the basics, you can modify them to your liking. In time, you may be able to achieve deep muscle relaxation using the 3-2-1 method, with 3 being the head, neck, shoulders, and arms; 2 the trunk of the body; and 1 the thighs, legs, and feet. Using the 3-2-1 method, you can take several "minivacations" of relaxation throughout the day.

Meditation

O nce physical relaxation has been sufficiently achieved, you can begin to quiet the mind through meditation. Meditation is as natural as sleeping, although it is quite different. In meditation, you are seeking a sharpened awareness; you journey deep within your mind to concentrate gently on a single, simple, even profound idea or concept. The process can move you to heightened understanding of yourself and a deepened faith in God found nowhere else. Again, meditation can be learned through many paths, all of which are constructed to bring peace and calm to a frenetic, chaotic, confused mind. The goal of meditation is to bring order, focus, structure, and above all, quiet and peace of mind to your thinking.

Start with a short relaxation sequence, then choose a word or phrase as your mental focus. Actually "see" this word or phrase in your mind's eye. It doesn't matter which word or phrase you choose, as long as it reminds you of peace and quiet. I recommend you use a word with spiritual significance for you, such as *Jesus* or *Holy Spirit* or *healing* or a short phrase such as *God heals.* You may choose a personal affirmation, such as *I am a child of God* or *God is with me always* or *God's power sustains and heals me now.* Any short sentence like this or any of the healing meditations that correspond to the thirty healing virtues discussed in Chapters Two through Seven of this book are quite satisfactory.

Once you become comfortable with focusing mentally on a word or short phrase, you can augment your experience by adding attention to your breathing. Focus on the air entering your body through the nostrils and filling the lungs from the abdomen up. Hold your breath for several seconds, and then simply let it go, ever so gently and effortlessly. As you let go, also let go of any extraneous thoughts that may invade your focus.

Always be full of care and appreciation for your body and of gratitude for your spiritual essence. Don't try to evaluate your thoughts or wonder "how am I doing?" Just let yourself "be" and move to the very center of your being. Let go and listen to the guiding, healing voice inside. Listen and you will hear the gentle whispers of eternity speaking psalms of truth, beauty, and goodness. You can practice this three times a day, but even once a day for about twenty minutes will bring rich rewards. Spending time with the Lord like this is spiritually bolstering and physically stabilizing; it can become your spiritual well of refreshment.

Prayer

Prayer, the spiritual action you take to bring you into connection with God, is an essential component in the healing process. Prayer provides a road that leads to healing. It melts any barrier separating you from God. Prayer manifests the warmth of the singular love that lies at the heart of your holy relationship with God's healing presence. Prayer is your conversation with God.

There are many forms of prayer. In prayers of petition or supplication, we request something of God. We give thanks to God in prayers of thanksgiving and offer praise and honor in prayers of adoration. We express our sorrow and ask for God's forgiveness in prayers of contrition. Some prayer types have evolved from various spiritual traditions, such as Benedictine, Ignatian, Augustinian, Franciscan, Thomistic, and Teresian. In addition, there are formal or vocal prayer, mental or meditative prayer, contemplative or centering prayer, scriptural prayer, and forgiveness prayer. All these forms of prayer are means of achieving the same goal: communion with God.

The form of prayer we are most concerned with in this book, of course, is healing prayer. We can pray directly for healing when we offer prayers of petition, asking God's help to become more virtuous. Generally, however, healing is like happiness; it is the marvelous by-product of pursuing our true spiritual identity with all our strength, might, and stamina. When we pursue God with everything that is within us, healing emerges like a spring, suddenly bubbling forth from parched earth. All prayer, then, is actually a form of healing prayer, since all prayer has as its central purpose greater closeness with God, our true source and center.

You may find the following books helpful in enriching your prayer life: *Prayer and Temperament: Different Prayer Forms for Different Personality Types* by Kodansha Ltd. and Marie C. Norrisey, *Prayer: A Handbook for Today's Catholic* by Reverend Eamon Tobin (Liguori Publications), and *Nine Ways to Reach God: A Prayer Sampler* by Bridget Meehan, SSC, D.Min. (Liguori Publications).

The following three-step procedure can be a powerful form of healing prayer designed to strengthen virtue within you:

1. Review a particular incident or situation in your life in which you feel that you acted in a nonvirtuous way. Try to picture the situation in your mind's eye in as much vivid detail as you can. Now try to actually relive the incident, not just remember it. Think what you thought then and feel what you felt. Recall the actual dialogue, the voice inflections, and the bodily postures of yourself and the other people involved in the incident. Run through the entire sequence of events in your mind just as you remember them.

2. Identify the main character trait you projected during this incident. Perhaps the easiest way to identify it would be to ask yourself, "Which virtue did I most violate in this scenario?" The opposite character trait from this virtue will be the trait or "vice" that pushed you to act in this nonvirtuous manner. It might be anger, envy, jealousy, fear, distrust, condemnation, or laziness. The important thing is to identify the exact trait you want to change.

3. Invite Jesus into the picture in your mind. Ask him to teach you how the entire incident or situation could be "replayed" using a healing virtue instead of the vice you originally embodied in the incident. Now go through the entire sequence again with

Jesus right there beside you teaching you how to act and what to say, using one of the thirty healing virtues as your guidance in the mental reenactment. As the scene in your mind's eye draws to a close, recognize the difference in how you feel toward the entire situation. You are not the same person you were before you entertained this modification. You are transformed; you are no longer vice-driven but virtue-motivated.

Prayer brings us to ever deeper levels of communion with God. Various forms of prayer stimulate us to recognize more clearly the many facets of our loving and healing God. Prayer allows us to see the goodness, mercy, and truth of Jesus, as well as to understand the Good News Jesus proclaimed in the New Testament. Prayer enables us to appreciate the Word of God, to seek new truths and to develop new insights into the nature of God and our wholeness with the loving force of the universe. Prayer motivates us to accept fully the gifts of the Holy Spirit that infuse our lives with grandeur and wonder. Finally, prayer offers us pathways by which we can transform the physical beauty of the world into testimonies of God's truth, beauty, and goodness. We regard our environment with a great *Amen* through prayer. Prayer is the spiritual balm that energizes the healing system inside us.

Imagination and Fantasy

Imagination brings figures, circumstances, events, and relationships into sharp focus in the mind. Imagination generally involves projecting into the future to "see" how you would like some future event to take place. Fantasy refers to placing yourself in another dimension and seeing yourself in a situation that is far removed from your normal lifestyle. There is great overlap between imagination and fantasy. However, imagination deals with the realm of the possible, or at least probable, while fantasy deals with the impossible. Let me give an example of each.

Let's say that you were planning to visit your sister, whom you hadn't seen for some time. The two of you haven't shared the best relationship over the years; indeed, you have held a grudge against her because of an incident that occurred a long time ago. Now you want to patch things up. You can imagine how you would like your visit to proceed. You can develop an image of the setting — your words, your feelings, and so forth. You can actually rehearse in your mind how you would like the reconciliation to proceed. This is imagination.

Athletes often use imagination to practice their sport. For example, a golfer may mentally image exactly how he or she would like to swing the driver and "see" the ball sailing straight toward the pin. Or he or she can mentally practice putting, imagining the ball gliding effortlessly into the cup. Research has shown that athletes who use imagination to augment their actual practice eventually perform better than those who do not. Here is the benefit of imagination: you can affect your behavior any way you would like.

Fantasy is similar to imagination but involves forming mental images that are outside the realm of physical possibility. For example, if you are struggling to achieve a greater understanding of God's presence within you, you can actually imagine yourself descending to the very center of your soul. You might imagine yourself sliding down a pole, descending successive flights of stairs, floating like a feather, or any other image to get you deep within yourself.

Once you do get there, you can form an image of what your soul looks like. Perhaps it's a beautiful chapel. Imagine yourself walking down the center aisle of the chapel and kneeling at the altar. Now imagine that you feel the weight of a hand on your shoulder. You turn to find Christ standing right next to you. He begins talking to you. What does he say? Now what happens?

You can even have fantasies about going inside your body, encountering your sickness in whatever form you imagine it to take, and then performing some healing procedure on it. Some examples might be straightening out a twisted bowel, unplugging a clogged artery, hosing away cancer cells, exploding a tumor, lubricating arthritic bone joints, peeling off head pain from the inside, or any of an infinite number of "procedures" you can perform for your own well-being. Naturally, these would never replace the actual medical procedure, but they can be emotionally strengthening as supplements and could even change the very chemistry in the laboratory we call your body.

As you can see, fantasies aren't idle daydreams or impractical reverie. Deliberately devising an appropriate fantasy allows you to tap into your very emotional and psychic core in a way that gives you peace and comfort and, consequently, healing.

Storytelling

Stories help you step outside yourself while at the same time providing the opportunity to identify with the characters, content, themes, and resolutions of the story. This identification process further empowers you to clarify feelings, formulate decisions, and, finally, take action. Stories allow you to roam around in your subconscious and resurrect complex material that ordinarily might not get out. Stories can provide you with much the same benefits as dreams. Your subconscious mind creates the setting and the situations necessary for you to "act out" your fears, guilt, repressions, and doubts. You can express yourself more clearly, if not more directly, by creating stories.

Stories need characters, plots, problems, tensions, and resolutions. Here you find the "stuff" of the human condition and a window into your wider being, your complex and largely unknown world, that needs airing. Here you can find answers to problems that conflict and confound the rational mind and give you a glimpse of your spiritual dimension.

The following story is designed to correspond to the perception function of the personality.

> Close your eyes and imagine this scene: In a cozy log cabin, deep in the forest, a glowing fire crackles in the fireplace. A father is sitting before the fire with his five-year-old child on his lap. The child is dressed in fleece-lined slippers, pajamas, and a flannel bathrobe. Father is wearing a red-checked flannel shirt and smoking a pipe.
>
> The father and child sip hot chocolate and munch on popcorn. They feel the penetrating warmth of the flames. Their cheeks are rosy from the heat of the fire. The pungent aroma of burning logs mingles with the comforting smell of the hot chocolate. They savor the taste of buttered popcorn and feel the smooth, slightly furry texture of flannel against their skin. The bright flames cast dancing reflections on the walls of the otherwise dark cabin, and burning logs hiss and crackle. Outside the cabin, the winter wind howls as it rattles the windows, and raindrops pulsate on the roof.
>
> Suddenly, the two are startled by a strange noise outside in the wind and rain. Father puts on his overcoat, boots, and hat, and tells the child that he will be right back after he checks to see what caused the noise.

At first, the child is confident and climbs back into the easy chair where the two had nestled just moments before. But as the time lengthens and the fire dies to embers, the child begins to feel chilled, not only because of the dying fire but also by a shiver of fear. The kerosene lamp Dad lit just before he left now dies from lack of fuel. The fire, now almost out, is the only light in the dim cabin. Fear is beginning to hang in the air like ominous icicles.

Somehow the child gathers the courage to walk slowly to the front window and pull back the curtain. Rain beats on the windowpane, forming a watery distortion that makes it impossible to see anything. The chill of fear now escalates to near panic. The swirling wind bumps the porch furniture to and fro, and a frantic feeling of desperation stings the small child, now all alone, cold, and empty. Feeling forlorn and forgotten, alone and fearful, the child begins to cry.

Suddenly, a new idea occurs to the child, "I am not alone. God is here with me always." Again, the child peers out the rain-slicked window, but this time…

You end the story.

As you can imagine, stories can be constructed around most any theme: sickness, healing virtues, the six functions of the personality, relationships, conflicts, or almost any aspect of the human condition. They needn't be long, complicated, or even particularly well constructed from a literary standpoint. They simply need to be relevant. Perhaps the most effective way of storytelling is in a group setting, where the participants can exchange stories and feedback. Stories are personally revealing regardless of how cryptic or shrouded they may seem. One cannot subtract the personal element from any creative endeavor.

Drawings

Dr. Bernie Siegel, who uses this technique extensively in his "exceptional patient" workshops, says, "The drawings are a wonderful way to get people to open up and talk about things they would otherwise conceal." Dr. Siegel asks patients to draw any scenes from their life that they like, but he especially asks patients to draw themselves, their treatment, their disease, and their own body's way of eliminating their disease.

Naturally, the technical quality of these drawings is not important (at least ninety-nine percent of the people whom I ask to draw are at first embarrassed by what they see as their artistic ineptitude). What is important is what the drawing portrays and how the drawing is interpreted. Drawings tap into the deepest part of our motivating forces. They may reveal material that has long been buried or that the patient is highly resistant to exposing in a rational, direct manner. Drawings may bring to light conflicts and dilemmas about which the patient had little, if any, conscious knowledge and even less understanding. Drawings are a marvelously effective means to unearthing new attitudes, perspectives, and beliefs that may not have found the light of day otherwise.

In group settings, drawings of any and all themes or directions are not only fun to do but also personally instructive. The fail-safe element of both storytelling and drawings is that all interpretations are given by the patient and are expressed in a tentative rather than conclusive manner, thereby skirting the sense of expertness which might otherwise emerge with professional interpretation. I encourage drawing, drawing, and more drawing, either individually or in groups.

Reminiscing

Reminiscing was once viewed by the mental-health community as the idle wandering of a diminished, or at least diminishing, mind. Today we recognize fully that looking back and remembering past events in our lives is not only healthy but fun as well. The positive aspects of reminiscing have been incorporated into a concept known as *life review*. Life review is a quite normal behavior that we all engage in. Life review enables us to see life patterns and to develop life understandings that may otherwise go unnoticed.

Memories from the past can be triggered by different stimuli. Pictures, objects, clothing, and writing (especially letters) can be wonderfully practical in helping people get in touch with their past. In addition, magazines, newspapers, newsreels, and other historical materials are likewise effective tools. Asking the person to relate remembrances or to keep a memories journal can give substance to what would ordinarily be but fleeting and unconnected thoughts. Calling to mind past events or examples of up-lifting incidents or elevating actions of virtuous living will brighten the individual doing the remembering and stimulate spiritual understanding of the present.

Persons who are seriously or terminally ill or who are in pain or discomfort need to reflect upon their lives so they may gain maximum worth and understanding from it. Their central developmental task is finding integrity; otherwise, they may slip into despair. Integrity means finding the patterns and themes of purpose and meaning that run through one's life. Integrity produces a sense that "My life has been okay. Yes, I might have changed a few things, but I recognize the presence of God throughout my life and I'm complete."

This book is dedicated to finding deeper, more profound meaning through becoming aware of God's work in our lives. Reminiscing can facilitate this great work by sparking memories of times when patients may see, with more accurate and spiritually enhanced hindsight, that God was indeed invested in their lives, although at the time they may not have thought God was there for them at all. Here is the recognition of the invisible hand of God manifest in the lives of his children. Here is the basis for spiritual development, faith enhancement, love extension, and hope advancement. Here is the true reality of our existence.

In addition to the techniques described above, I have developed *Generations...the game,** which enables individuals and groups to expand and enrich the life-review process. Life review is so effective for positively addressing depression on the worldly plane and for injecting spiritual meaning into events previously recognized as ordinary human behavior that I wanted to ensure that families had a vehicle for practicing life review in a comprehensive and fun manner. The game has proven invaluable in any group situation where persons wish to address their lives in a growthful, Christian way.

---

* For information about *Generations...the game*, write to the author at the address given on page 160.

Sentence Completion

Sentence completion is a unique and challenging but eminently productive means of generating material from your belief core. It is disarmingly simple, yet dramatically effective and motivating. It consists simply of identifying a theme or issue and constructing an appropriate sentence stem. For example, suppose you wanted to investigate the role of the virtue of hope in your life. You would start with the sentence stem "If I could exercise the virtue of hope in the way that I'd like to, I would..." Now your job is to come up with six to ten sentence-completion statements. Your sentence completions might be something like

"If I could exercise the virtue of hope the way I'd like to, I would...
- be much closer to God.
- be secure and serene.
- be friendlier and more optimistic.
- understand myself better.
- recognize the goodness of God's presence in my daily life.
- not worry so much.
- be able to forgive more easily.
- not be so angry.
- not feel so sick to my stomach.
- facilitate healing in my body.

Of course, these are just examples, but they do illustrate how the multiple sentence-completion technique can generate a large amount of data very quickly.

Upon analysis, these sentence completions are usually enlightening and may motivate action. The benefits of the sentence technique is that you are moved from confusion to clarity very smoothly and quickly. This clarification greatly expands and drives the decision-making function of the personality, especially if you take the next step in the technique, which is another sentence stem in which you use the sentence completion statements you have already generated. Here's how it works:

You would begin with the sentence stem "In order to be much closer to God I would have to..." This stem is a real action motivator. When you can complete this sentence, you have successfully bridged the gap between vague and unexamined beliefs, perceptions, thoughts, and feelings and gone directly to the decision and, hopefully, on to the action steps.

You can use the sentence-completion technique with almost any topic or issue that you can think of. It is particularly helpful when trying to find applications for the thirty healing virtues in your daily life. For example, the tenth healing virtue is "simplicity/beauty." You might start with the sentence stem "If I could use simplicity/beauty in the way I'd like to, I would..." Another sentence stem might be "Some ways that I could incorporate simplicity/beauty into my life would be..." Either of these two stems would help you generate completions that provide great insight into possible decisions and actions you could take in your life right now. Taking the technique one step further, once you have generated six to ten sentence completions, you can use them to make sentence stems that push you even deeper into your belief core. The process is simple but flexible and effective. I recommend it highly.

Support Groups

There has been a veritable explosion of support-group formation in the United States in recent years. Many reasons have been cited for this expansion, among them the pent-up need among people for community and connectedness. This social need is nowhere better demonstrated than in the many groups that have been spawned through Alcoholics Anonymous, or AA. The Twelve Steps of AA have been applied to nearly every human malady. Support groups exist in the AA tradition for problems dealing with gambling, overeating, anorexia, parenting, drug abuse, aging parents, cancer pulmonary, and heart disease — the list goes on and on. The popularity of the support-group movement is testimony to the success they have generated among God's people.

Support-group involvement can pay handsome dividends for participants. First, groups lend mutual support. We all need words of encouragement, empathy, and guidance. Persons facing the same turmoil and discomfort that we face are in a facilitative position, since they are intimately familiar with the problems we endure. We attach greater meaning to their words and actions than we would to the words and actions of those not privy to our personal trials.

Second, groups generally provide practical education. Whether this information is provided through organized presentations or through informal interaction in the group process, education is going on all the time in a well-run group.

Third, groups tend to lessen guilt, sorrow, or unhappiness and generally enhance our confidence to continue in the face of our burden. Whatever the disease, misfortune, or calamity, we need both to express our innermost feelings and to develop determination to carry on.

Fourth, groups teach techniques and skills we need to live the most self-actualizing lifestyles we can. Modeling is perhaps the premier teaching and learning technique demonstrated in a support group. When we see our fellow group members using skills and competencies that seem successful for them, we will be more motivated to adopt them for ourselves than we otherwise would.

Fifth, groups are resource centers for information dissemination. The various members of the group pool their respective information of the many resources they have used, along with evaluative comments about how successful this particular resource was for them.

Sixth, groups provide "affirmation of self" to each member. Groups facilitate personal growth through interpersonal communication, positive feedback, security, and affirmation of action. A collective and encouraging, if unspoken, "You're doing all right!" seems to swell up among the members of the group that bolsters the overall self-reliance of each member. (See Appendix "Training for Support Group Facilitors" for more on support groups.)

These ten techniques are solid and reliable means of helping yourself or others tap into the healing power within. This list is not exhaustive. There are many other techniques, but these ten can be used with confidence. I recommend that you keep a journal of your spiritual thoughts and feelings, which can serve as your spiritual/healing growth treasury.

I wish you God's love, her nurturing peace, and his sustaining strength. Amen.

Appendix

TRAINING FOR SUPPORT-GROUP FACILITATORS

Support groups are not normally led by professionals, although they certainly can be. A professional is a person trained in aspects of mental health and knowledgeable about group dynamics and group process. This kind of in-depth training is usually unnecessary. What is required is a person who understands human nature, can communicate with above-average ease and precision, is nonjudgmental, and has knowledge of the particular issue that serves as the purpose for the group. Beyond that, group facilitators could well use the following personal characteristics: courage, willingness to model, emotional presence to the group, goodwill and caring attitude, belief in the group process, openness, ability to cope with possible criticism, personal power, stamina, willingness to seek new experiences, self-awareness, a sense of humor, and inventiveness. While not exhaustive, this list is fundamental. These characteristics are generally not learned from formal training but are more often gifts the person has been given as part of the overall personality.

In addition to the above characteristics, support-group facilitators require some skills to be maximally effective. These skills include active listening, reflecting of feeling, clarification, summarization, facilitation skills, empathy, positive interpretation, questioning, linking, confronting, supporting, blocking, diagnosing, reality testing, evaluating, and terminating.

A thorough explanation of each of these thirteen characteristics and sixteen skills is beyond the scope of this book. However, the author offers training sessions that not only define the above characteristics and skills but also train facilitators in the maximum use of the nine other techniques of healing in a group situation covered in this chapter. Facilitators will receive training in how to organize and teach an eight-session Healing Virtues Workshop based on the principles and techniques in this book. The author has constructed a pencil-and-paper instrument that measures the degree to which an individual has incorporated each of the thirty healing virtues into his or her life. This instrument, the Healing Virtues Profile (HVP), is an integral part of the workshop. The workshop is intended to precede participation in a Healing Virtues Support Group.

Support groups for those suffering from any kind of physical or emotional brokenness can be formed and profitably executed in a variety of settings including your own church, hospitals, schools, retreat houses, nursing homes, retirement centers, senior centers, adult daycare centers, senior housing complexes, and many other locations where people congregate. I heartily encourage you to think seriously about starting a Healing Virtues Support Group in your locale. The benefits to you in your own growth path can be absolutely phenomenal. Good luck!

For further information about Support Group Facilitator Training or about *Generations...the game,* contact

Richard P. Johnson, Ph.D.
Center for Ministry Transition
1714 Big Horn Basin
Wildwood, MO 63011-4819
(636) 273-6898
Web site: www.SeniorAdultMinistry.com
E-mail: drjohnson@lifelongadultministry.org